THE

SPACE
ECONOMY

A Guide for Investors, Entrepreneurs, and Aspiring Professionals

THE

SPACE
ECONOMY

CAPITALIZE ON THE GREATEST BUSINESS
OPPORTUNITY OF OUR LIFETIME

CHAD ANDERSON

WILEY

Published by John Wiley & Sons, Inc., Hoboken, New Jersey.
Published simultaneously in Canada.

For general information on our other products and services or for technical support, please contact our Customer Care Department within the United States at (800) 762-2974, outside the United States at (317) 572-3993 or fax (317) 572-4002.

Wiley also publishes its books in a variety of electronic formats. Some content that appears in print may not be available in electronic formats. For more information about Wiley products, visit our web site at www.wiley.com.

Library of Congress Cataloging-in-Publication Data is Available:

ISBN 9781119903727 (Cloth)
ISBN 9781119903970 (ePub)
ISBN 9781119903987 (ePDF)

Cover Design: Courtesy of Ethical Design/Space Capital
Cover Images: © Golden Sikorka/Shutterstock, © David Lugasi/Dreamstime
Author Photo: © David Noles Photography

SKY10045490_041023

Space is for everybody. It's not just for a few people in science or math, or for a select group of astronauts. That's our new frontier out there, and it's everybody's business to know about space.

—Christa McAuliffe,
American teacher and astronaut (1948–1986)[1]

Contents

Acknowledgments

Writing a book involves plenty of solitary work, but no project of this scope is completed without the generous help of many brilliant and accomplished people.

First off, heartfelt thanks to my esteemed colleagues at Space Capital, who have contributed greatly to my current understanding of the growing Space Economy and our advanced investment thesis: Tom Ingersoll, Justus Kilian, Paula-Kaye Richards, and Jia Cheng Yu as well as the world-class experts who constitute our Operating Partners: Aaron Zeeb, Jonny Dyer, Dirk Robinson, and Tom Whayne. I'm so grateful to be working with such extraordinary allies.

A special thank you to the portfolio company founders who shared their precious time and invaluable perspectives from the front lines of innovation: Dan Ceperley, Lucy Hoag, Sid Jha, Nathan Kundtz, Dan McCleese, Robbie Schingler, James Slifierz, and Anastasia Volkova.

Next, I would like to thank Marc Ventresca, my University of Oxford professor, who equipped me with frameworks to understand how nascent markets develop, prepared me to recognize the significance of SpaceX back in 2012 and its parallels to other nascent market catalysts, and empowered me to pursue this market opportunity well before it was obvious.

Thanks to the many pivotal industry leaders who were so generous with their time, helping me accurately portray the structural changes and key milestones that gave rise to the entrepreneurial space age: Mike Griffin, Scott Pace, Peter Marquez, and Lori Garver.

Thanks to David Moldawer for helping me wrangle my ideas into book form. Also, thanks to the world-class publishing team at Wiley: Jess Filippo, Debbie Schindlar, and the team at Cape Cod Compositors. Thanks also to Ethical Design in Sydney, Australia, for their excellent work on the book's cover. Above all, thanks to my editor, Richard Narramore, who first approached me about writing this book. (Great idea, Richard!)

Finally, but also firstly, I'd like to express heartfelt gratitude to my wife, Radhika, for her love and support during the writing process.

Introduction

If you're reading this, you probably have the sneaking suspicion that something big is on the horizon. You may even have glimpsed a harbinger of this coming change: small, low-Earth orbit (LEO) satellites swooping across the sky, parts of the rapidly growing satellite constellations powering the global economy to a greater extent each day.

We use the term *Space Economy* to encompass every business that relies on orbital access to deliver its value, from Planet Labs,* a company imaging every inch of the ground from space on a daily basis, to Pokémon GO, a hit mobile game that works using GPS signals from satellites.

(An asterisk will mark the first appearance of any company Space Capital has previously invested in.)

For all the media coverage of SpaceX* and its iconoclastic founder, Elon Musk, commercial launch services are just the beginning of the story. The Space Economy is much more than rockets and satellite hardware. Space-based technologies are next-generation digital infrastructure, the "invisible backbone" of the largest global industries. Most people have yet to grasp the genuine, world-changing business implications of lower-cost orbital access. CNBC has called space "Wall Street's next trillion-dollar industry."[1] Bank of America predicts that "the growing space economy will more than triple in size in the next decade to become a $1.4 trillion market."[2] Morgan Stanley expects a space-based business to create the world's first trillionaire.[3]

Humanity has operated in space for decades, but, for reasons covered in Chapter 1, only recently has space become a category for investment. Given that this entrepreneurial space age is only a decade old, most of the action is still in the private markets, but we're beginning to see some companies listed on public markets where retail investors can participate. If you think back to the late 1990s, there were a handful of publicly traded technology stocks. Seemingly overnight, "technology" became an investable category to diversify your portfolio. Today, that label has lost its meaning. Every company is a technology company. Space is in the same position that tech was then. One day, "space" as a label will lose its usefulness as every company begins to rely on space-based technology in some way to deliver value.

Space technologies have already delivered massive returns for investors. GPS is a space-based technology that has generated trillions of dollars in economic value, as well as some of the largest venture outcomes in history. As we'll see in Chapter 1, GPS provides a useful playbook for understanding how other space-based technologies will create new investment opportunities across the economy. Two of these—Geospatial Intelligence and Satellite Communications—already play critical roles in most major industries, including agriculture, logistics, telecom, and financial services.

There was a time when terms like "e-commerce" and "blog" began appearing regularly in magazines and nightly news shows. At the time, these bits of unfamiliar lingo were whimsical curiosities to the mainstream, newfangled phenomena relevant to teens, scientists, oddballs, and geeks but of only momentary interest to everyone else. How soon the internet changed things—as much for magazines and news shows as for every other business. Few people understood the scope of that onrushing change, let alone how to harness its potential. Of those who did, you know more than a handful, from Reid Hoffman (Netflix) to Jeff Bezos (Amazon) to, once again, Elon Musk (PayPal).

Chances are a warning bell has been going off in your mind about all the recent interest and activity in space. While you may know something noteworthy is happening, the full implications are still hard to see. This book will give you the lens you need.

Let's say you're a serial entrepreneur, or that you're entertaining the notion of starting something of your own. As a founder, why risk entrepreneurship if you're not going to shoot, literally, for the Moon? Or, at least, in that general direction? Even if you already see the opportunity in this rapidly growing market, however, you have questions: For all the investment capital flooding into the Space Economy, is there any interest in what I can offer? Do I have the necessary qualifications? Do I need a background in avionics or engineering? Should I have worked at NASA first? Will I need to bring a personal fortune to the table, as Elon Musk did with his proceeds from selling PayPal?

The answer to all these questions is a resounding no, but these concerns and others will be addressed in detail here.

Likewise, you may be an investor curious about the potential of these new businesses and industries but unsure how to measure their value—or weigh their risks. How much of this stuff is *really* happening, as in, likely to turn a profit over the next few years? And which of these new businesses are still *Star Trek*, not *60 Minutes*, despite the assurances of scientists and entrepreneurs? Investors have heard a lot of hype from space "experts" over the last few years. This book will help you separate fact from science fiction.

We're at an inflection point. What's actually happening in space is more astonishing and otherworldly than all the breathless promises of the space crazies, the wild-eyed talking heads who keep promising a Starbucks on Mars by early next year. Fifty years ago, the first glimmers of a global computer network containing all the world's knowledge attracted scant public interest. Meanwhile, jetpacks inspired awe and wonder even though people regularly flew on airplanes. Would jetpacks really have been more important than the World Wide Web? Of course not. To the average person in 1973, however, jetpacks were easier to understand. The same goes for the genuine potential of today's Space Economy. It's more difficult to grasp than the idea of a Mars-based latte, but it's well worth the effort of doing so.

To succeed as an investor in any category, you need to understand not only fundamentals like profit and loss but also the lay of the land where you plan to allocate your resources:

the companies and their customers. The markets and the major players. Consider this book your manual and your map. As investors and operators, the team at Space Capital brings a unique combination of in-house technical expertise, entrepreneurial experience, and an investment track record to the table. There is no predicting the future, but some guesses are far more grounded than others. Read on for ours.

If you're not an entrepreneur or an investor yourself, you may be a professional seeking a role in the Space Economy. In fact, you may already be working in a space-related industry, anywhere from incumbent defense contractors to new heavyweights like SpaceX and Planet Labs to one of the many space startups that have been founded over the last few years alone. As a leader, manager, or frontline employee, you will find a wealth of valuable information here, including lessons and advice from CEOs, veteran space industry professionals, space policy experts, visionary technologists, and more. The diversity of perspectives this book provides will give you an unparalleled look at the big picture, along with many actionable takeaways.

***

Here I go, making big promises about the future, just like all those people preselling caffeine on the Red Planet. Why take my word on any of this?

After managing a $50-billion real estate portfolio through the Great Recession, I decided to seek a greater purpose than investment banking. I wanted to make a genuine, lasting impact on the world. Drawn by its Skoll Center for Social Entrepreneurship, I went to Oxford University to earn my MBA at the Saïd Business School. There, I had the opportunity to learn from the brilliant economic sociologist Marc Ventresca.

Ventresca, an authority on technological innovation and market formation, taught me all about the nascent markets that spring up from innovative breakthroughs like the car, the PC, and the mobile phone. In Ventresca's class, I learned what nascent markets look like and how they evolve. Just before I matriculated at Oxford, on May 24, 2012, SpaceX had successfully delivered cargo to the International Space Station (ISS) aboard its Dragon capsule, a first in commercial spaceflight. It would be hard to imagine a more fortuitous piece of serendipity: Learning about market formation, I could see recent evidence of the birth of a bona fide new market.

By successfully completing its ISS cargo mission, SpaceX had done the unthinkable, achieving a feat previously restricted to three world superpowers. Where things went next seemed obvious to me. Market competition would increase efficiency and decrease prices. More and more businesses would be able to participate in the Space Economy. All kinds of unforeseen products and services would crop up. Fortunes would be made (and lost).

At the time, I felt certain I couldn't be the only person who saw a market forming. SpaceX wasn't operating in secret, after all. Musk delighted in trumpeting every milestone on social media. As early as 2003, he declared an unambiguous parallel between space and the internet: "I like to be involved in things that change the world. The Internet did, and space will probably be more responsible for changing the world than anything else."[4] Here was a serious tech entrepreneur telling everyone that outer space was "where the future is." Surely, now that Musk had delivered on the promise of an ISS cargo mission, entrepreneurs and venture capitalists around the world would scramble to leverage affordable orbital access. I'd have to work quickly if I wanted to participate.

Recognizing that all the new space startups I envisioned would need venture capital, I decided to start an early-stage investment fund specializing in the category. To be successful in such a deeply technical field, however, my background in finance wouldn't be enough. So, as a first step, I sent a cold outreach email to the CEO of Astrobotic,* a Pittsburgh-based space-robotics company making progress toward Google's now-defunct Lunar XPRIZE. In my email, I offered to help

Astrobotic develop a market assessment for commercial lunar transportation services, pro bono. Astrobotic agreed, and I spent the next nine months working closely with them to study the emerging opportunities around Lunar transportation and infrastructure.

This was my first experience working within the Space Economy itself, interacting not only with the team at Astrobotic but also with other leaders in the field. To my surprise, I found that nearly everyone working in the Space Economy (as I'd already begun to think of it) was either an engineer or a scientist. There were no MBAs and very few general entrepreneurs. Maybe there was room for me after all.

The report I ended up writing, the first assessment of its kind, generated attention for Astrobotic, which even used it to pitch NASA. (Though the Lunar XPRIZE ended after a decade without a winner, Astrobotic went on to win hundreds of millions of dollars in Commercial Lunar Payload Services contracts and is due to send its Peregrine lander to the Moon aboard United Launch Alliance's Vulcan Centaur rocket by the end of 2022.[5]) Meanwhile, in exchange for my contribution, I received an invaluable understanding of this new market.

After Oxford, I published several academic papers on related topics. One explored the ramifications of the ISS cargo run, explaining how public–private partnerships had made commercial spaceflight economically feasible and arguing for the real, near-term economic potential of space technologies.

"The docking of Dragon represented a historic moment where a commercial enterprise managed to achieve that which had previously only been accomplished by governments," the paper read.[6] What I'd written went on to be cited widely, but I was just getting started. There's a difference between research and application, and I wasn't just studying the Space Economy. I wanted to help build it.

In 2013, there was close to zero private activity or investment in the Space Economy outside of SpaceX. Despite my sense of urgency, I seemed to be one of the few people on the business and investment side who saw this as an opportunity. (In Chapter 6, we'll look at the troubled history of the commercial space industry and how prior failures led many to miss the turnaround when it finally happened.)

Without enough deal flow or investor interest to support a fund, I helped stand up an innovation center focused on the commercialization of the United Kingdom's space sector. At the Satellite Applications Catapult, I incubated and accelerated startups and mobilized investment in space businesses. Working at the Catapult, I built my professional network and cultivated a reputation within the field. At night—work hours back on the East Coast—I built Space Capital. Lacking sufficient capital to invest, I leveraged my expertise and the unique data set I'd gathered to educate and inform the market, combat misconceptions, and help investors understand where things might be headed.

By 2015, I had enough momentum to raise seed capital. Moving to New York City, I established Space Capital's headquarters and, in April of that year, launched our inaugural SPV (special purpose vehicle) fund, collecting money from groups of individuals to, at first, invest in Planet Labs. These weren't blind pools of venture capital. They were funds I'd cobbled together myself, deal by deal. I'd find an opportunity, do the due diligence, and bring it to the investors directly.

That December, SpaceX achieved a successful landing and recovery of their rocket, ushering in greater reusability and further reducing the cost of reaching orbit. This feat catalyzed sufficient investor interest to launch Space Capital's first institutional venture capital fund in 2016. At that point, I knew it was time to bring in a partner. I needed someone who would complement my finance background with heavy-duty industry experience and technical expertise. Unfortunately, I found that many of the people visibly operating at the intersection of space and business were . . . overly enthusiastic. Or, to put it bluntly, hucksters. Venture capital is a reputation business. I couldn't afford to associate myself with a snake-oil seller. I needed to ally with a serious businessperson with a deep background in space. Making a list of candidates, it soon became clear that Tom Ingersoll was the person I needed to meet.

At the time, Ingersoll had been advising blue-chip venture capital funds on commercial space opportunities. As a CEO, he had already led two successful exits of venture-backed space businesses, making him one of the most accomplished opera- tors in the Space Economy. As an engineer and entrepreneur, Ingersoll had an impeccable pedigree, vast industry experi- ence, and enough expertise on the investing side to meet me halfway. You can imagine my delight when he agreed to join Space Capital as my fellow managing partner.

Tom Ingersoll started his career with a decade-long stint in the Phantom Works advanced prototyping division of McDon- nell Douglas, the legendary aerospace company that eventually merged with Boeing. There, Tom worked with Apollo astro- naut Pete Conrad on several key projects, including the Delta Clipper Experimental (DC-X), a reusable single-stage-to-orbit launch vehicle.

In 1996, Tom co-founded Universal Space Lines with Pete Conrad, T. K. Mattingly, and Bruce McCaw. Ahead of its time but with a grand vision to become an operating company for the burgeoning commercial space industry, Universal Space Lines founded two subsidiaries: Universal Space Network, a pro- vider of commercial tracking, telemetry, and control services for spacecraft, and Rocket Development Company, a commercial launch company.

A decade later, Ingersoll, with the help of McCaw, led the sale of Universal Space Network in one of the earliest successful exits in the Space Economy. (Now a subsidiary of Swedish Space Corporation, the network Ingersoll helped build has been instru- mental in scientific missions in both LEO and Lunar orbit, as well as for commercial satellite services like Sirius XM.)

Next, Ingersoll was brought in to lead Skybox Imaging, a company developing satellites to provide frequent, reliable, high-resolution imagery of the Earth. In 2014, he led the sale of Skybox to Google for $500 million in one of the largest venture-backed exits in the Space Economy at the time. (Skybox was later acquired by Planet Labs, where its assets are a key revenue driver.)

With the sale of Skybox behind him, Ingersoll stepped back for a look at the overall landscape. While more investment capital was flowing into commercial space efforts than ever before, too much of it was heading into "the wrong places." That's why the timing couldn't have been better when I reached out to him about Space Capital.

"People were making claims they couldn't achieve," Ingersoll told me. "It wasn't healthy for the investment environment. It made me nervous. Space Capital was a way I could make a difference by steering money away from the space crazies. If people aren't making money in space, capital will dry up."

Today, Ingersoll believes the space-crazy tide has turned: "Things are absolutely going in the right direction. There's froth, and some bad investments are always made, but we're on a great trajectory in general. There are better insights. There are more serious investors entering the picture."

Soliciting Tom Ingersoll's participation in Space Capital has easily been one of the best decisions I've made with the firm. There are few people on the planet with his soup-to-nuts technical and operational experience in the commercial space industry. Few but him have brought not only spacecraft but entire space businesses from seed to success not once but several times. Tom's expertise and intelligence are an invaluable part of Space Capital's value proposition, and I count myself lucky to call him my partner. Without a doubt, it's the talent we've assem bled that explains why top-tier venture capital and private equity firms consistently look to us for operational guidance.

At Space Capital, we are experienced fund managers and operators, deeply embedded in the Space community, with a strong technical understanding. Our partners have built rockets, satellites, and operating systems. We have founded companies with assets currently in space and have led multiple exits as operators. We have been investing in this category for over a decade, and top-tier venture capital and private equity firms have consistently looked to our partners for operational guidance. As thesis-driven investors, we attract the best founders, ask better questions, and make better decisions.

You may wonder why a company that trades on its expertise would share its knowledge in a book. As I said earlier, before I had a cent of capital to invest, I used my expertise in the Space Economy to educate and inform the broader market. Investor education is still an integral part of our strategy. This book joins a wide array of Space Capital white papers, blog posts, podcast episodes, and television appearances. As investors, we believe that, for all the activity in today's Space Economy, the world is nowhere close to fully embracing the exponential growth opportunity at hand. With orbital access for all within reach, there are so many ideas and innovations from other industries that can now be applied to space. In spreading our insights, we hope to spur greater participation in the Space Economy by the most talented entrepreneurs, investors, and professionals.

Over a quarter of a trillion dollars has been invested into nearly two thousand unique space companies over the past decade alone. Simultaneously, public interest in space-related careers has surged: Space Talent, our space-focused talent community and job board, currently lists 30,000 open positions across 700 companies. The Space Economy is here, and its growth is trending almost straight up.

As of this writing, orbital launches are on a record pace for the year, led by SpaceX and China's state-run launch operators. There were 72 launches in the first half of 2022. If that pace continues, we will break the record of 135 successful orbital launches set in 2021.[7] Much is happening, but if you rely on mainstream news that touches on space and space-based technology, it's easy to miss the forest for the trees. Stories that touch a nerve generate clicks. As we've seen across the media landscape, this distorts the picture.

Some businesses in the Space Economy are making real progress toward genuine and lasting improvements to our quality of life, from reducing pollution to ensuring our food supply, but they're succeeding in ways that are hard to summarize for a general audience. Other businesses wow a gullible press with flashy and dramatic promises but pursue approaches that aren't grounded in good science.

It's a complex and powerful story like this one that demands a book-length treatment. The Space Economy isn't something you'll understand from reading the latest headlines. It's too easy to confuse recency with relevance. Keeping up with space-related posts on the tech blogs alone won't clue you into what's really going on. To understand today's Space Economy, you need a balanced, fact-based perspective with enough context to understand the implications.

At Space Capital, my partners and I spend most of our time talking to companies about their goals. Crucially, however, we follow up by doing our homework. We validate assumptions and estimate odds based on the facts. The reason we've been so successful is that we have the requisite expertise and investment experience to dig deeply into even the most technologically ambitious entrepreneurial vision.

At Space Capital, we know most of the key figures operating within today's Space Economy. Over the years, we've talked shop with many of the leaders, government officials, technologists, and innovators driving progress in space, and I have also conducted a series of dedicated interviews specifically for this book. Backed by these incredible outside contributions, I feel confident that *The Space Economy* will stand for some time as the most comprehensive and authoritative look at this exciting field.

***

The book is comprised of 10 chapters, each of which is designed to stand alone as a comprehensive resource on one or more key facets of the Space Economy.

The first chapter defines the Space Economy lens and makes the case that space is about much more than just rockets and satellites. As you'll see, the next-generation digital infrastructure provided by satellites is becoming part of the foundation on which every part of our economy—retail, shipping, manufacturing, *everything*—depends, unlocking a universe of new possibilities and changing the world in profound ways.

Chapter 2 offers a map of today's Space Economy, explaining the different categories we've identified and highlighting some of the key players. One of the most interesting things about the Space Economy is just how much incredible innovation is going on outside the spotlight. Companies are already finding product-market fit and generating tremendous amounts of value in this arena, and my hope is that a better understanding of the playing field will help you understand where you might make your own contribution.

Chapters 3, 4, and 5 offer targeted advice for founders, managers, and leaders of companies within the Space Economy. Whether you're an entrepreneur toying with an idea that relies on space-based technology like GPS, the leader of a small but growing application developer using Earth Observation (EO) data in novel ways, or the CEO of a satellite manufacturer on the verge of an IPO, you will find valuable advice here from an array of major figures in the field combined with our own observations, insights, and best practices at Space Capital.

The Space Economy is unusual in how closely it interfaces with government organizations and policymakers. In addition to an in-depth exploration of the evolution at NASA that led to the success of SpaceX and the birth of the Space Economy, Chapter 6 offers an insider look at the current rules around space and how they are likely to evolve in the near future. If your company operates in space or plans to do so, this chapter is required reading.

Chapter 7 offers practical guidance and useful insights on separating fact from fiction when it comes to space-based tech and making the best possible use of your funds to generate robust, resilient, long-term growth in any portfolio with a space-aware investment philosophy.

If the idea of working within the Space Economy excites you, you're in luck. The opportunities go far beyond specialized areas like physics and engineering. In Chapter 8, I walk through the most in-demand skills, traits, and attributes of space professionals and offer guidance on pursuing the most promising career paths. There's room for everybody, and best of all, the Space Economy will be incredibly resistant to downturns.

In the aftermath of COVID-19 and the Great Resignation, talent has become the most pressing challenge for nearly every organization. This is doubly true within the Space Economy, where the competition for talent is even fiercer than in the tech industry as a whole. On the bright side, great employees are drawn to ambitious companies with inspiring missions. Space Economy businesses are the most ambitious on the planet. In Chapter 9, I cover what the smartest organizations are doing to attract, develop, and retain world-class talent.

Most of this book is devoted to the here and now: the Space Economy as it currently stands and the opportunities waiting for anyone smart and ambitious enough to seize them. That said, there is value in looking a little further ahead, in this case at the Emerging Industries of the Space Economy. Lunar bases and crewed missions to Mars really aren't as far off as you might think, and those possibilities represent just a fraction of the potential that some very smart and highly pragmatic leaders have in mind for the next few decades. In Chapter 10, I offer a down-to-earth, hype-free, reality-based overview of what is likely to come next, as well as a look at the far-fetched ideas you can safely dismiss as highly improbable. I'll also look at two existential threats—climate change and military conflict—and explore the dangers and, more important, hopes offered by the Space Economy.

In highlighting the exciting potential of the Space Economy to change the world for the better, my hope is that people on both sides of every political divide can come together and work toward a vision for a healthier and more resilient world. Elon Musk may be planning humanity's exit strategy via Mars, but until then, there's plenty worth saving here on Earth. We finally have tools that offer the promise of a way forward.

It's with all this in mind that I call this the most important book you can be reading right now. *The Space Economy* will serve as a crucial primer for understanding where things are really headed—not just in the United States, not just across the satellite industry, but throughout the economy as a whole—and positioning yourself within it as an investor, an entrepreneur, or a career professional.

Wherever you stand, this story affects you. Are you going to learn more about this new reality and seize the opportunity for all it's worth? Or will you play it "safe" and stick your head in the sand? A new world isn't just coming. It's literally on the launchpad. Take-off is imminent. Are you ready to board?

CHAPTER 1

Space Is the Next Big Thing: To See the Future of Your Job, Your Investments, and the Economy, Look Up

I f you've ever wished that someone from the future had tapped you on the shoulder and told you to invest in Apple Computer in 1983, found an e-commerce company in 1996, or take a risk on that Google gig in 2002 instead of playing it safe at Bear Stearns, you understand the importance of distinguishing signal from noise. It's as crucial for personal success as it is for commercial satellites.

The pattern repeats throughout history: As a new wave of opportunity builds, a handful of people position themselves to ride that wave to its crest and prosper. The rest of us watch them rise and wish for time machines.

No one is born with the ability to see through the hype and zero in on what's really next. The winners earn their edge through the accumulation of knowledge and insight. Read on to join their ranks.

***

To understand the scope and potential of the Space Economy, look at the rise of a now-ubiquitous space-based technology: the Global Positioning System (GPS). The story of GPS and how it has fundamentally changed the world will help you grasp the far greater potential of the Space Economy as a whole.

On September 1, 1983, a Soviet fighter plane shot down Korean Airlines Flight 007 en route from New York City to Seoul, South Korea. A navigational error had sent the Boeing 747 passenger plane into Soviet airspace at a moment of peak Cold War paranoia. Within minutes, missiles had been fired at what the Soviets believed to be a reconnaissance aircraft for the West. In all, 269 civilians were killed.

In the wake of the tragedy, Ronald Reagan declared that GPS, a technology being developed for military use, would be made available to all as a public good. Whether or not the KAL 007 tragedy spurred this move or simply offered Reagan a timely moment to announce a decision that had already been made, this technology that had been created for warfare would soon help everyone find their way. The world would never be the same.

A 2019 report commissioned by the United States Commerce Department estimated that GPS has created $1.4 *trillion* in economic benefits in the United States alone since the system became publicly available in the 1980s.[1] Today, this crucial layer of infrastructure continues to enable new technological applications. As of 2020, free access to location data has driven exponential business growth worldwide, creating nearly 800 companies with a combined equity value of over half a trillion dollars. The importance to the global economy of this invisible signal cannot be overstated. The world relies on GPS and other global navigation satellite systems (GNSS) for everything from plotting local driving routes to coordinating the supply chain. Uber, Yelp, and Niantic, creator of Pokémon GO, rely on GPS to function and together represent some of the largest venture outcomes in history. According to the PitchBook financial database, the top 25 exits through 2020 for GPS-based companies have generated an average exit multiple for the earliest investors of 690×. Even if you aren't an experienced investor yourself, you can surely appreciate a return of 690× on an investment.

For all its importance and still-untapped potential, GPS is only part of the story, one of three space-based technology stacks within the Satellites industry that unleash extraordinary value every day. These three stacks represent a next-generation digital infrastructure that underpins multitrillion-dollar global industries today. More on all three stacks later. For now, the story of GPS helps frame the discussion to come because GPS itself is a familiar, incredibly valuable technology, yet one so ubiquitous as to be almost invisible. The lens that brings GPS into focus will help you see the potential of the Space Economy as a whole.

The Birth of a Market

In 2012, as the commercialization of space was getting underway, the Space Economy exhibited all the key characteristics of a nascent market on the verge of dramatic growth. SpaceX, Elon Musk's California-based vehicle manufacturer and launch provider, had sent its Dragon capsule to the International Space Station (ISS), where it delivered cargo and supplies before returning safely to Earth. Previously, only three government superpowers—Russia, China, and the United States—had berthed a spacecraft at the ISS and brought it back successfully. That year, a private company joined their ranks, and in a way that would quickly enable the entrepreneurial ambitions of others. Classic market lift-off!

In business-school speak, technological innovation follows an S-curve. At first, progress is incremental and haphazard as the idea is driven forward in fits and starts. As marketing expert and author Geoffrey A. Moore put it in his book of the same name, "crossing the chasm"—spreading an innovation from the early adopters to the mainstream—is extraordinarily difficult even in the ideal case, when the new thing is clearly superior to the old one. Many promising technologies fail to make it across the chasm at all. Many more take an extraordinarily long time to do so.

From unexpectedly high costs to regulatory roadblocks to the defensive maneuvers of entrenched incumbents, there are many factors that can slow the spread of an idea. A crucial piece of technology may still be missing from the value proposition. Or there might be a small but pivotal flaw in the design just waiting to be noticed by a subsequent entrepreneur. Sometimes, the obstacle is cultural inertia, and all that's really missing is a tenacious entrepreneur willing to deliver the needed push.

Whatever the barrier might be, the fall of that final obstacle spurs a rush of early adopters to take the plunge. If the product or service rewards their enthusiasm, they spread the word, giving birth to a new market and unleashing a wave of subsequent entrepreneurship and innovation. Exponential growth follows. The S-curve heads upward.

Eventually, the pent-up potential of an idea diffuses into the marketplace. Once the late majority and laggards—for example, your parents—are on board with the new product or service, growth plateaus once more. An "S." Then, over time, the once-revolutionary innovation reaches the limit of its usefulness or competitive advantage. Newer ideas arise, and one of them crosses the chasm, too, rendering the previous innovation obsolete. Goodbye vacuum tubes, hello transistors.

In the case of the Space Economy, several factors throttled progress prior to 2012. Before SpaceX, the process of getting something into orbit was not only difficult and dangerous but also convoluted, expensive, and opaque. This made launch a bespoke, low-volume business. As a satellite manufacturer, you would fly halfway across the world to meet with a Russian launch provider for several days to discuss requirements. Then, you'd go home and wait. Eventually, you'd be summarily informed of the cost of your proposed launch: $130 million, or $90 million, or $300 million. Why one number and not another? No one knew. Pricing was essentially a black box. Getting an object into space meant that money had to be no object. This meant that you were either a government agency, a major telecom, or a defense contractor. The opacity alone represented a formidable barrier to entry—how do you raise capital when you can't say how much capital you need to raise?—and this was only one of several major barriers that needed to come down for the Space Economy to flourish.

Iterating with software is relatively fast and cheap. Speedy iteration isn't possible with mega-infrastructure projects led by government agencies, defense contractors, and telecoms. Unfortunately, those were the only players for decades. Since space wasn't accessible for the average Fortune 500 company, let alone aspiring entrepreneurs, the market was essentially closed to new entrants, which meant that big, ambitious ideas—the kind newcomers bring—were few and far between. For innovators, space was a dead end. Why pursue an idea with no affordable way to test and iterate on it? Better to focus your energy and creativity on an iPhone app.

SpaceX made the process of accessing orbit not only more affordable but also transparent, publishing their pricing for all to see. Once entrepreneurs could develop business plans based on real launch costs, they could raise capital. No more hazy estimates from close-door committees in a Russian conference room. Today, if you have a solid founding team and a promising idea that leverages launch, you've got a good shot at funding.

As we'll see, SpaceX's next launch vehicle, *Starship*, will make getting to orbit even more accessible. But it was its *Falcon 9* rocket that started the snowball rolling, fundamentally changing the economics of space.

Thanks to economies of scale, smartphones have drastically lowered the cost of processors, sensors, and other electronic components, even as quality and capability have skyrocketed. Before SpaceX, however, satellite engineers were restricted to using components with "space heritage": tech that had been used successfully in space, even if it was completely obsolete by consumer standards. Likewise, as every other industry took advantage of storing and processing data in the cloud, satellite data remained locked in private server farms, accessible only through expensive, manual, and frustratingly bureaucratic processes.

Once SpaceX tipped the first domino by bringing the cost of launch down and making prices transparent, it became feasible to send an array of smaller, cheaper, and more sophisticated satellites to space instead of one big one. If a single small satellite fails, you have plenty of others as backup. This had the effect of releasing decades of tech innovation in one go by giving engineers the freedom to rely on off-the-shelf components that were both cheaper and more capable than those with space heritage. Similarly, new satellite operators entering orbit aboard a Falcon 9 enjoyed the convenience of piping data into the cloud rather than investing in banks of new servers. This shift spurred the incumbents to follow suit, opening up a vast trove of satellite data to new applications.

The final barrier blocking growth in the Space Economy was access to capital. That's where Space Capital and its peers enter the picture. When I founded the firm, there was essentially no venture capital activity focused on the Space Economy. Once the market opened up to new entrants with viable shots at growth, the equity investment started flowing. See Figure 1.1.

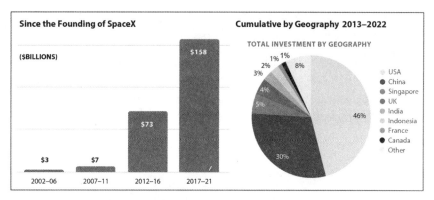

FIGURE 1.1   Private Market Equity Investment in the Space Economy

How Did We Get Here?

The Moon landing was the greatest technological feat of the twentieth century. Fifty years later, the United States was the dominant world power, and yet it lacked any launch capacity of its own. With the retirement of the troubled Space Shuttle program in 2011, America was forced in a twist of historical irony to rely on the Russians to get its own astronauts to the ISS. It was a humiliating nadir for the "winner" of the so-called Space Race to rely on the "loser" for launch.

Equally surprising, it fell to a prickly South African tech entrepreneur to execute one of the most dramatic technological turnarounds in history, dragging the United States from laggard to leader in the space sector in under two decades.

As someone who has observed SpaceX's trajectory closely, I can say that Elon Musk's success has felt like anything but an overnight one. Yet Musk has persisted. His reasoning is clear: "The future of humanity, it's going to fundamentally bifurcate in two directions," Musk said in an interview. "[Either] it's going to become multi-planetary, or it's going to be confined to one planet until some eventual extinction event."[2] Even when things go south—and SpaceX as a company has dealt with its share of hurdles—this mission keeps the company going.

"When something is important enough," Musk told *60 Minutes* not long after the Space Shuttle program ended, "you do it even if the odds are not in your favor."[3] Today, SpaceX is tipping those odds.

In Chapter 6, we'll learn more about why America's launch capabilities faded—and the key factors behind their resurgence.

Gauging the Size of the Opportunity

Inexpensive orbital access is a momentous change, but does it have real-world implications for investors, entrepreneurs, and aspiring professionals? Starting a space infrastructure company like SpaceX's Starlink is still more difficult and expensive than buying a cheap laptop and programming a mobile app. As we'll see, however, most of the Space Economy's economic potential for today's entrepreneurs lies in leveraging the data provided by satellites with new software applications. Even solo entrepreneurs successfully bootstrap businesses like these, no giant hangar required. The economic potential of the Space Economy is unquestionably open to all. The real question is, how can one identify and leverage the emerging opportunities being unlocked while staying cognizant of the risks of any new market?

Many factors contribute to success, timing chief among them. For example, Beal Aerospace was a well-capitalized private company that tried to be SpaceX before SpaceX. In addition to facing technological problems, however, Beal failed to break the defense contractors' stranglehold on government contracts. By the time SpaceX arrived on the scene, in contrast, the political conditions were more favorable. Could SpaceX have succeeded in Beal's place? Hard to say, but there is no question that the timing was better when it did enter the fray. Likewise, the Emerging Industries of the Space Economy—from Mars bases to asteroid mining—will have their day, but that day is not today. Don't let far-off possibilities distract you from real-world opportunities that are viable right now.

Entrepreneurs pitch us all the time with ideas that are not just overambitious but flat-out physically impossible. We're pretty good at spotting these because, as discussed in the Introduction, Tom Ingersoll and other key experts at Space Capital have built rockets, satellites, and operating systems, founded companies with assets currently in space, and led multiple exits as operators. Our track record and accumulated expertise are why Space Capital remains a trusted source of operational guidance for top-tier venture capital and private equity firms.

You need to do your homework to win. Nascent markets like the Space Economy are exciting, dynamic, and fast-moving, but they are also prime breeding grounds for hucksters and bottom-feeders. Simply surveying the field—in part, by reading this book—will inoculate you against many of the hazards. With the benefit of hindsight, it's clear that people get swept away by things that are obviously too good to be true because of willful blindness. All of us want in on the Next Big Thing, whether we're choosing a career, an investment opportunity, or an entrepreneurial niche to explore. Understand that about yourself and stay cautious. Anyone can make a prediction, but if you can't get a clear and reasonable explanation of *why* a given opportunity is worth your time, money, and attention, pass on that opportunity or gamble with all three.

This book offers a way of thinking about the opportunities currently orbiting above us. Think of it as a map for understanding this chaotic landscape of innovation and opportunity, one that, as we'll see, encompasses areas as varied as AI and climate tech. I aim to convince you that the Space Economy is the right lens for bringing the greatest opportunities of our era into focus. Today, several space technologies sit in the same part of the S curve as GPS did back in the 1980s when far-sighted companies like Trimble, Magellan, and Garmin brought an obscure, satellite-based positioning system from the military to the mainstream.

People always get the pace of technological progress wrong. When a new innovation arrives, we all imagine wild possibilities just around the corner. When those breakthroughs don't arrive immediately, however, we quickly become cynical and stop paying attention. Meanwhile, out of the public eye, that nascent innovation keeps evolving, slowly at first but faster and faster until progress not only meets those early expectations but exceeds them. We've reached this inflection point with the Space Economy. Are you paying attention now?

Why Now Is the Right Time to Launch

The Space Economy saw record-breaking levels of investment in 2021. Then came headwinds: the lingering effects of COVID-19, the war in Ukraine, the changing climate and its consequences—mass migration, disease, famine—and the end of the longest market bull run in history. This is to name just a few of the calamities keeping business leaders (and everyone else) up at night. Global challenges like these require global solutions.

In times of uncertainty, information becomes even more important. As the sky falls, businesses and governments only increase their investment in space-based data. Earth's orbit offers an unparalleled vantage point to gather and transmit knowledge about the state of the world. There is no substitute for a view from above. Today's space technologies constitute an invisible backbone powering the world's economy. GPS, as well as two other satellite technology stacks—Geospatial Intelligence (GEOINT) and Satellite Communications (SatCom)—play a crucial role in most major industries, doing everything from tracking fugitive methane emissions to optimizing global shipping routes. It's for these reasons and more that the Space Economy will be countercyclical. In boom times, space-based data helps businesses expand. In times of crisis, it keeps them resilient.

The term "Space Economy" may evoke the "space tourism" of companies like Blue Origin and Virgin Galactic, companies that launch "cashtronauts" to the edge of space. The near-term, hold-it-in-your-hands potential of space-based technology, however, is far better illustrated by Planet Labs. Planet Labs was started in 2010 by a group of former NASA engineers who realized that NASA's quintuple-redundant, ultra-resilient approach to satellite design no longer made sense in the era of SpaceX. Why spend enormous amounts of time and money building a single, practically infallible satellite when you can launch a swarm of cheap and tiny ones that operate as a distributed network? If a few satellites fail, there are still plenty more to keep the network operational. Advances in consumer electronics mean that low-cost, off-the-shelf components originally developed for cars and phones can be used to build satellites with more advanced capabilities than the most sophisticated traditional options.

Planet Labs was one of the first pioneering companies to fully take advantage of more affordable launch services. The company was also our first investment at Space Capital, though, by the time we got our fund up and running in 2015, the company was already raising Series C growth capital. Since 2017, Planet Labs has had a network of small satellites imaging the entire planet daily. Its stock is now traded on the New York Stock Exchange.

Planet Labs is just one example of what is now possible. As major innovations—the steam engine, the transistor, the laser—have always done, SpaceX has spawned an entire ecosystem of startups around it. Opening up orbit is unlocking the future.

Just How Big Is Space?

On November 15, 2021, the seven astronauts onboard the ISS were warned to seek shelter in case the station was damaged by an oncoming cloud of debris.[4] Without warning, Russia had tested an antisatellite weapon (ASAT) by blowing up a defunct Soviet satellite weighing nearly 5,000 pounds, releasing hundreds of thousands of pieces of debris into Earth's orbit in the process and endangering everyone onboard the station—including two cosmonauts. One of the more surprising parts of this bizarre occurrence was that private companies in our portfolio did a better job tracking the explosion and its consequences than the U.S. government.

Later on, after it began its invasion of Ukraine, Russia rumbled threats about shooting down foreign satellites using its ASAT weapons. The commercial space industry was throwing a wrench in its usual modus operandi of controlling the flow of information out of the warzone. Civilians worldwide could track the progress of invading troops through traffic reports on Google Maps. Russian efforts to shut off Ukrainian communications and shape the public narrative through propaganda became even harder when SpaceX shipped Starlink terminals to Ukraine to help its people stay connected and coordinate military operations.

Just as America's Operation Desert Storm was the first GPS war, the invasion of Ukraine is the first space war. The economic, political, and now strategic importance of the Space Economy can no longer be denied. This is why we are seeing such exponential growth. In the first quarter of 2022 alone, more than $7 billion was invested into 118 space companies, bringing total private capital investment into the Space Economy past the quarter-trillion mark. Three-quarters of the action is taking place in the United States and China, but activity is rising nearly everywhere else, from New Zealand (Rocket Lab*) to Japan (iSpace) to Finland (ICEYE*). The Space Economy is increasingly international and the arena is open to all.

Between 2012 and 2021, private capital fueled innovation across almost 2,000 unique companies that span the three satellite technology stacks—GPS, GEOINT, and SatCom. Each of these stacks comprises three layers: Infrastructure, Distribution, and Applications. The Infrastructure layer is the hardware and software involved in building, launching, and operating space-based assets. The Distribution layer is the hardware and software involved in receiving, processing, storing, and delivering the data from those assets. The Applications layer is the hardware and software that uses this data to deliver products and services to customers. For example, Lockheed Martin launches GPS satellites (Infrastructure) that generate positioning and timing data. Companies like Trimble and Garmin make terminals (Distribution) that receive GPS signals from satellites. Software developers like Uber, Yelp, and Niantic write software (Applications) that relies on GPS data. Distribution companies like Garmin and Applications companies like Uber are part of the GPS stack even though they play no role in the GPS satellites themselves.

Much of the growth in the Space Economy we've witnessed over the past decade has been based on what is now a 10-year-old launch paradigm. With the arrival of SpaceX's enormous, fully reusable Starship—more on the significance of this revolutionary launch vehicle later—we will enter a new phase of development, one that will further accelerate the pace of growth and enable entirely new industries. The Space Economy promises viable solutions to the most pressing and urgent problems of our time, from resource scarcity to climate change. The faster it grows, the better.

The Rise and Fall of America's Space Ambitions

The Germans' V-2 was the first long-range, guided, ballistic missile, as well as the first human-made object to enter space. In 1944, a V-2 crossed the Kármán line, an altitude still roughly considered to be the boundary between Earth's atmosphere and outer space. One hundred kilometers above mean sea level, the Kármán line is, by definition, one that no propellor craft can cross because the air becomes too thin to generate lift.

After World War II, the German engineer Wernher Von Braun and a small army of his fellow experts were brought to the United States as part of Operation Paperclip. There, the creators of the V2 helped the United States develop its own rockets and, in 1958, its first satellite: Explorer 1. Eventually, Von Braun, a former SS officer, became director of the new Marshall Space Flight Center, where he led the development of the Saturn V vehicle that sent the Apollo missions to the Moon. America saw the quest to dominate space as so important to its future that it gave Von Braun and his colleagues access to the country's most secret sites and projects.

If Operation Paperclip were the only game in town, progress might have run more slowly. In fact, we might still be working toward a first Lunar visit. However, the 1,600 or so German expats who swore allegiance to America were solidly outnumbered by the 2,200 scientists and engineers that the Soviet Union relocated within its own borders. Once the two great powers were chasing the same prize with their own secret reserves of German rocket experts, every space-related brass ring carried the weight of national pride. Every milestone became an argument for an economic system and a political worldview. Which model drove progress faster: capitalism or communism?

In retrospect, the Space Race between the United States and the Soviet Union can't be understood along economic lines alone. The idea that a program like Apollo was somehow crucial to America's national security feels like a thin justification when you consider what that money and effort might have accomplished if it had been invested in nuclear weapons or deterrents. Instead, both countries invested enormously in chasing each space "first," from the first satellite in orbit to the first human on the Moon, while investing little thought in what would come after all those momentous firsts had been achieved.

The Soviets took an early lead in this game of orbital one-upmanship. Spurred by the Americans' stated intention to launch a satellite, Russia launched Sputnik 1 first, in 1957, stunning the globe. Explorer 1, the Americans' first satellite, launched the following year, but no silver medals would be offered by the public. It was a stinging defeat. More firsts followed for the Soviet Union: Laika, the first mammal in space (1957), Luna 1, the first spacecraft to leave Earth's orbit (1959), Luna 2, the first spacecraft to land on the Moon (1959), Yuri Gagarin, the first human in space (1961). Maybe the lead came down to the 600 additional German experts Russia had secured for itself. Regardless, the Soviets left the Americans scrambling. Their brutal, no-holds-barred approach to progress seemed justified by their extraordinary results. Something dramatic would have to happen to make the case for the American Way.

In 1962, John F. Kennedy addressed a nation that had been set back on its heels. Speaking in front of 40,000 people at Rice University, the young president made the case for landing Americans on the Moon among other space-related feats "not because they are easy, but because they are hard." By that point, Kennedy had already told Congress of his intention to fund a Moon landing—Von Braun believed this was the next brass ring to chase—but lawmakers had offered a chilly reception to the idea, and it wasn't hard to see why. Polls showed a majority of Americans against the landing: Too expensive. Too risky. The government ought to focus on Earth's problems instead. Former President Eisenhower called the idea "nuts." However, Kennedy's impassioned and eloquent speech, addressed directly at America's image of itself, turned the tide of public opinion.

One forgotten element of Kennedy's plan was that he hoped to cooperate with the Soviet Union on the Lunar landing. Apparently, Nikita Khrushchev eventually warmed to the possibility.[5] At the least, it would offer Russia a valuable glimpse at the latest American technology. Unfortunately, Kennedy was assassinated before Russia's cooperation could be secured, and the idea was swiftly dropped by the next administration. America would capture this brass ring—or fail to do so—on its own. And America did capture it, on July 20, 1969, when the *Eagle* lander touched down on the surface of the Moon, and Neil Armstrong and Buzz Aldrin became the first humans to step foot on our nearest celestial neighbor. Five similar missions to the Moon followed, with the last, Apollo 17, putting Eugene Cernan and Jack Schmitt on the surface.

It's been over half a century since Cernan and Schmitt ascended from the Lunar surface, yet no human being has returned to the Moon. If you want to understand how the United States could accomplish this extraordinary feat only to gradually turn its back not just on the Moon but on space exploration in general, you can point to several important factors: Economic turbulence. The 1986 *Challenger* disaster. Systemic problems with how NASA paid its contractors. All these practical considerations and more will be discussed in detail in Chapter 6. However, it's possible that the underlying reason for our fading space ambitions was the assassination of JFK in Dallas on November 22, 1963. Kennedy's life and presidency were cut short before he could architect a long-term, economically viable vision for America's space program. Once the narrowly defined goal of a crewed Lunar mission was achieved with Apollo 11, there was no leadership at a national level around where America should go from there. As the post-war boom faded and the American economy began to sputter in the 1970s, investing in space seemed less like an engine of growth and innovation than a distraction from urgent concerns "down here." In light of the economic value space technology is currently delivering, it's hard to imagine a more flawed and damaging misconception, but at the time, space felt very far away.

Emblematic of America's cooling space ambitions was the Space Shuttle program. In a matter of years, the country lurched from running ambitious missions named after Roman gods like Apollo and Mercury to operating a "shuttle" to low-Earth orbit (LEO). In the national imagination, NASA became a glorified Port Authority. This impression of obsolescence and irrelevance was only underscored by ballooning budgets, sporadic meaningful accomplishments, and an increasingly problematic record of failures and accidents. When NASA retired the troubled Shuttle program in 2011 without a replacement, it left the country with a major gap in capability. In the press, however, the end of the Shuttle registered as little more than a historical footnote, a faint reminder of a more ambitious age.

An Unexpected Resurgence

Not long ago, NASA operated under a system riddled with waste and failure driven by counterproductive, short-sighted incentives. Pretty much like any other large American government bureaucracy, in other words. If NASA wanted a rocket or satellite built, it went to a small group of defense contractors and paid one of them a vast sum of money to go build it according to a fixed set of specifications. These were known as "cost-plus" contracts. The contractors figured out pretty quickly that they could make more money by dragging things out than by getting the job done on time and under budget. If they spent years and billions working toward a critical objective without much progress, they could go back to the trough for more money: "This engineering stuff is tougher than we'd expected," they'd tell the bureaucrats. "We need two more years and X billion more dollars to finish the job."

Under a cost-plus system, NASA had little choice but to agree. It could pay more and get what it needed, eventually, or it could scrap the mission altogether. NASA's ability to negotiate was further restricted by planetary launch windows that appeared only periodically. If you're wondering why American space innovation stagnated in the 1980s and 1990s, look no further than cost-plus. The government wasn't a customer of the defense contractors; it was their benefactor. Ultimately, these companies weren't funded to get the job done efficiently but to keep large numbers of constituents employed.

Thanks to some very smart leaders at NASA whom we'll meet in Chapter 6, a new, more robust system was established in the

2000s. Under a "fixed-price" system, NASA identifies the service it wants: "Develop the capacity to get this many people and this much cargo to the ISS on this schedule." NASA tells the marketplace: "If you can do it within this price range, you are guaranteed payment." If a contractor meets NASA's requirements, it can count on a guaranteed revenue stream. If it goes over budget, that's its problem. This system of incentives finally made real competition possible. A 2020 report from the U.S. Government Accountability Office to Congress concluded that "a firm-fixed-price contract . . . provides maximum incentive for the contractor to control costs and perform effectively and imposes a minimum administration burden upon the contracting parties."[6]

Fixed-price contracts were the kick the Space Economy needed. Competition cuts costs, increases efficiency, and drives innovation. When multiple providers compete under commercial terms, the customer—NASA—reaps the benefits: lower costs, faster development, more contractor accountability, and stronger mission assurance. By fixing its incentives, NASA allowed SpaceX and other new entrants to flourish.

The full story of SpaceX lies outside the scope of this book, although we will touch on more elements later on. For now, it's enough to understand what makes the company so important to the Space Economy. Price transparency allows smaller businesses and startups to calculate costs, draw up realistic business plans, and secure funding for space-based projects. This has had dramatic effects, the success of Planet Labs being one early example. Simultaneously, bringing the cost of launch down by an order of magnitude through partial reusability opened the door to venture capital. As a consequence of lower prices, a tremendous amount of investment has poured into the Space Economy.

On the horizon, SpaceX's new launch vehicle, Starship, will take things to another level entirely. Built primarily from stainless steel and requiring few rare or expensive materials in its construction, Starship, for all its technological sophistication, exhibits a design philosophy more in line with commercial jets than NASA launch vehicles. It's intended to be cheap to produce, cheap to operate, and *quickly and completely* reusable. Imagine airfares in a world where airline employees tossed the plane into the ocean and rolled a fresh one out of the hangar after every arrival. Innovation would be glacial and air travel would be restricted to the ultrarich.

Capable of landing on and launching from Earth, the Moon, and Mars, Starship opens up a vista of new possibilities. Think about all the things you might do with a pressurized box, 1,100 cubic meters in volume, that can be sent to the Moon and back affordably. Today we measure space cargo in kilograms. Starship can carry *100 metric tons*. That's the equivalent of 150 large, male elephants, a thousand-percent improvement over a Falcon 9, which is already the option to beat. Whereas one seat on a Falcon 9 rocket costs about $75 million today, Musk is confident that an entire Starship launch will cost less than $10 million.

Starship will change everything, but it'll take time for most of us to understand just how profound this change will be. For example, given the vehicle's performance and cost, the standard strategy of optimizing for mass or size with price as no object will no longer make sense. Forget hugely complicated, inefficient, and ultra-redundant space stations. Theoretically, Starship can be refueled in orbit indefinitely. Fill it with equipment and crew quarters, and it's a DIY space station. Heck, throw in Egyptian cotton towels and some tasteful branding, and it's a Space Marriott. Load Starship up with machinery, and it's a zero-gravity microchip factory. Interested in a tour of the Moon? No need for bespoke Lunar equipment when you can tote along a few customized Humvees and some repair equipment. Roll the cars out the back of the vehicle and you're cruising to Copernicus crater. John Deere tractors might one day clear the plot for the first Moon base.

Starship will fundamentally change how we operate in space. With its first full-scale orbital test flight expected in 2023, Starship will further remove the barriers to entry and stimulate

the development of entirely new applications. Space exploration has stagnated for decades. Today, commercial capabilities
are quickly outpacing those of governments. NASA, American
defense contractors, and other major players like China are
being forced, at long last, to play catch-up.

Space Is International

By this point, you may have noticed an American tilt to the narrative. This reflects the fact that the United States sparked the
Space Economy and still dominates it—for now, anyway. We
aren't privy to many details about China's space plans here in the
West but, for one example, a Chinese national company, China
SatNet, is building a 12,992-satellite constellation in LEO.[7] This
is a large, serious effort to provide broadband internet access for
the Chinese, one they'll need since Starlink use is prohibited in
the country.

   Together, America and China account for 75 percent of
today's Space Economy, but exciting things are happening in
other parts of the world. For example, New Zealand's Rocket Lab
and Equatorial Launch Australia are two of the international
launch providers sending payloads into space regularly. Location matters greatly for launch, and no country has a monopoly
on the ideal conditions. Australia's Arnhem Space Centre offers
"excellent weather and stable upper atmospheric conditions; low
aviation and maritime traffic, a stable geo-political environment
and comprehensive logistics infrastructure."[8] Every country
brings its own set of advantages to this marketplace, and there
are exciting examples of Space Economy businesses from other
nations throughout the book. The story of the Space Economy is
increasingly an international one, and our investments at Space
Capital reflect that. However, an enormous amount of potential remains untapped. I'm writing this book in part to inspire
entrepreneurs, investors, and professionals in every country to

participate to the greatest possible extent. We all have an opportunity to participate in this new market.

***

A major part of our investing thesis at Space Capital is how we define the Space Economy. We believe that any technological product or service that depends on orbital access in some way belongs under this umbrella. Our definition causes consternation in some—what, people ask, does Uber have to do with outer space?—but, as you'll see, this is the only framework that fully captures all the potential that affordable launch makes possible. In the same way that every company today is a technology company, every company of tomorrow will be a space company.

We've already learned about the Infrastructure, Distribution, and Application layers within the GPS tech stack. Where GPS blankets the world in positioning signals that help us navigate, Geospatial Intelligence, or GEOINT, shows us, via sensor-laden satellites, exactly what we'll find there, wherever "there" happens to be. GEOINT Infrastructure companies handle the satellites, GEOINT Distribution companies process and serve the data, and GEOINT Applications use that data in increasingly useful and surprising ways.

Satellite Communications, or SatCom, encompasses the transfer of data from one place to another, embodied most visibly by the constellation of Starlink satellites that will soon offer wireless, uninterruptible, high-speed data access to every point on Earth, from Death Valley to the peak of Mount Everest. Once SpaceX's Starship launch vehicle makes it possible to rapidly launch the remainder of Starlink's 4,000-satellite network, you will *always* have a good signal. No matter where you go, there you are . . . watching Netflix.

See Figure 1.2: This matrix, summing up today's Satellite industry, neatly encompasses more than 90 percent of the value in the current Space Economy. Launch accounts for a few percentage points. Emerging Industries, discussed in Chapter 10, account for

FIGURE 1.2 Satellites: Largest of the Six Industries in the Space Economy

less than one percentage point. Both are important parts of the picture, but at Space Capital, we believe this sturdy little three-by-three matrix will stand the test of time as a framework to understand the big picture of the Space Economy—and envision new possibilities within it. Models are powerful tools for thought.

It's ironic that the Launch industry itself barely registers as a blip relative to what launch makes possible everywhere else. SpaceX's financial value isn't based on its launch operation, which amounts to a few billion dollars in annual revenue, but on the potential of Starlink. Likewise, the four Emerging Industries—Stations, Lunar, Logistics, and Industrials—are on the horizon but still small enough to consider a footnote. The big picture is what matters most, and that picture is getting very big indeed. In 2021, the Space Economy represented a solid 3 percent of *all* global venture capital investment, and is growing quickly.

I'll go into each part of the satellite technology matrix in greater detail in the next chapter. Meanwhile, I hope it's clear that space-based technologies are on their way to becoming an intrinsic part of our technological infrastructure, a layer below all the other layers even as these satellites soar high above us in greater and greater numbers. The possibilities of space are vast, but they begin right here on the ground.

CHAPTER 2

Mapping the Space Economy: Understanding the Ecosystem and Its Key Players

In this chapter, you'll find a map of the Space Economy as it stands today, along with a glimpse of its possible future. Understanding the big picture will help you frame and organize everything you discover in subsequent chapters. Before we go deeper, however, it's important to understand a crucial component of the growth cycle of new markets: unbundling.

When a company tries to spur the adoption of a new technology, it faces a chicken-and-egg problem: The steam-powered locomotive, for instance, isn't much use without rails. Nor is the telephone without telephone wires. So which piece comes first? And who builds what?

To get things started, the company that introduces an innovation usually builds all the complementary pieces required for that innovation to function. This bundled technology stack—trains, tracks, train stations, rail yards, signaling equipment, and so on—is an essentially unavoidable hurdle for first movers. Call it the first-mover *disadvantage*. Building a train is very different from laying miles of railroad track, yet a single company must do both simultaneously to achieve lift-off.

Bundled products and services are rarely as good as they might have been if each one had received the full attention of a dedicated organization. Nor do bundles serve every niche equally well. It's simple triage—the first mover must move quickly if it wants to capitalize on its opportunity before rivals steal its thunder. Once mass adoption of the innovation takes hold, however, other companies can enter the market by specializing in a single part of the bundle. By focusing, they can do it better than the incumbent does—or at least differently, better suited to a particular niche, for example. *Unbundling* a tech stack is an inevitable stage in the growth of any new market, yet it is often stymied by the first mover's lobbying efforts, trade group interference, and other monopolistic attempts to retain control of the most lucrative parts of the stack.

The rise of all-electric cars shows unbundling in action. For these vehicles to replace traditional cars entirely, they will need charging stations at regular intervals along every road, not just at strategic points in major cities. Tesla got the ball rolling with its network of Supercharger stations, but independent charging station operators are the ones making ubiquitous charging access a viable, near-term possibility.

This unbundling process is happening throughout the Space Economy. In the past, a Geospatial Intelligence (GEOINT) company would handle everything in-house: designing and assembling satellites, operating them in orbit, collecting their data with its own array of ground stations, storing imagery in its own servers, and selling the images directly to customers. A bundle like this leaves no room for competition and creates no incentive for the company to improve its offering beyond meeting the very specific demands of its existing customers, namely, government agencies. Obviously, it's impossible for a single company to do all these things well, let alone equally well for every potential customer.

A tightly controlled bundle is a competitive moat once you've built it, but the need for one makes entering the market very tough for newcomers. Planet Labs, mentioned earlier, ran head-first into this first-mover disadvantage. The founders simply wanted to launch and operate small, low-cost satellites for Earth Observation (EO) purposes but soon realized they would need their own ground stations and servers as well. Also, since they intended to sell to businesses that hadn't used satellite data before, they found themselves in the business of educating the industry about their product.

Thanks to a massive amount of effort, Planet Labs managed to cross this hurdle. Since then, the GEOINT stack has begun to unbundle. Going forward, companies will no longer need to build everything themselves. Startups and large companies alike are stepping into the Distribution and Application layers of the stack, making it possible for Infrastructure companies to focus on the satellite manufacturing and operations that are their core competencies.

Now that you understand how unbundling works and why it's so important, let's begin mapping the Space Economy with a look at launch, the fundamental challenge of getting mass into orbit. After all, launch is what makes all three satellite tech stacks possible.

Launch

When it comes to outer space, it's easy to pay too much attention to the rockets themselves. All that sound, light, and heat is hard to ignore. But launch providers have only attracted 9 percent of overall Space Economy investment over the past decade. The giant vessels created by the engineers at SpaceX and, to a lesser extent, Rocket Lab and other manufacturers represent only a small part of the story. By rapidly reducing the cost of orbital access, these companies have spurred a global wave of entrepreneurship and technological innovation. Rockets are relevant mainly in terms of what they make possible.

Most of the market value of SpaceX derives not from its launch business but from the long-term potential of its Starlink satellite internet network. One day, rockets—whether manufactured and operated by SpaceX or another provider—will be fungible commodities, just as swarms of fast-moving, LEO satellites will be ubiquitous in the night sky. A sea-change—space-change?—is underway. Don't believe me? Consider the closest technological parallel: the cargo container. A complete history of the cargo container lies outside the scope of this book. But there is no question that the twentieth-century development of a standard, rugged, and reusable box that can be packed with nearly any good and seamlessly moved between train, ship, and truck has transformed the world's economy in ways too numerous to count.

Prior to the cargo container, loading a ship was a slow, difficult, dangerous, and expensive undertaking involving the manual labor of an army of stevedores and longshoremen. At the dawn of the cargo container era, in 1956, "it cost an average of $5.83 per ton to load a cargo ship," according to Kathryn Schulz in *The New Yorker.* "With the advent of the shipping container, that price dropped to an estimated sixteen cents."[1] Today, shipping companies load vessels of staggering size with everything from cars to coconuts and deploy them across the ocean with incredible speed and minimal human involvement. Look up from this book at the environment around you, and you will find yourself surrounded by evidence of the cargo container, from that bowl of fruit to the computer on your desk to the desk itself. Oh, and the book, phone, or tablet you're holding, of course.

Next-generation launch vehicles like Starship will have a similarly dramatic effect on the cost of getting into orbit and, as a consequence, our daily lives, transforming our relationship with space even as the vehicles themselves become as dependable—and therefore invisible—as the common elevator. No drama and very little waste, just another piece of industrial equipment designed to move heavy things from one place to another.

Today, the astronaut holds special sway in the public imagination, but that romantic image harkens to an earlier era when entering orbit represented an extraordinary feat of talent, training, bravery, and determination. Like that of the cowboy, however, the mythic ideal of the astronaut is entering its twilight. As space launches, already computer controlled, become more frequent, routine, and reliable, launching into orbit will become about as dramatic as driving to Cleveland. The romance may be going, but personally, I'm far more interested to discover what this shift will make possible in every other area of our lives than cling to the past. Let's look at some concrete examples of what orbital access is already enabling.

Satellites

A pattern repeats itself throughout the history of astronomy and space exploration: An observation or discovery leads to an insight. That insight spurs technological innovation. Innovation breeds opportunity. Opportunity attracts entrepreneurs, who form a new market. From celestial navigation, lenses, and telescopes to Velcro, memory foam, and solar panels, space has long been a source of scientific inspiration and a driver of technological and economic progress.

Today, innovation is flourishing across the Space Economy thanks to the three satellite technology stacks introduced in the previous chapter: the Global Positioning System (GPS), GEOINT, and Satellite Communications (SatCom). Two developments unleashed the consumer potential of the three stacks: First, Google Maps, which, though it only launched in 2005, is already an essential part of daily life for most of us. (Dirk Robinson, one of our operating partners, led the team that expanded this extraordinarily useful platform.) Second, the iPhone 3G that Apple introduced three years later. This was the first consumer phone with built-in GPS. These two products transformed our collective relationship with location while unleashing the trillion-dollar industry of location-based services like Yelp and Uber.

Though it took a few years for these tools to upend the marketplace, we now live in a world in which everyone with a phone knows exactly where they are and where they're going at all times. It is also a world in which private companies can pay for a glimpse at the same information, for good and ill. This is still a new development in the grand scheme of human history, the implications of which are only beginning to be felt. Even so, another revolution of potentially even greater magnitude is on its way: more secure, more precise GPS paired with computer vision that will allow for accurate positioning in all three dimensions. This will unlock new applications in Augmented Reality (AR) that promise to change our lives in ways we can't imagine.

In offering the following overview of the three satellite technology stacks, it's my hope that you find yourself inspired. Learning about what is already possible, you may spot an investment opportunity, a new career, or even a new category of business as yet undreamed of by another human being, visible only in the outline of its absence from the map.

GPS

Space and navigation have been linked from the start.

More than 400 light-years away, two stars orbit a third. Together, these three celestial bodies stand out to the naked eye as a single, bright point of light. Since this point—Polaris—lies almost directly "above" Earth's axis, it appears fixed in place from the perspective of the Northern Hemisphere. This northern-oriented marker has helped us navigate since at least late antiquity. Through an accident of galactic billiards, three colossal balls of flaming gas serve as our trusty North Star.

Polaris has never been situated precisely to the North—its position is always shifting relative to Earth's axis. As our understanding of celestial mechanics improved over the centuries, navigators improved at accounting for Polaris's endless but minute circling of the North Pole. Meanwhile, there are many other stars that have been used to navigate, particularly across the open ocean. It was our study of space that unleashed trade—and conquest—on a global scale.

Today, of course, Polaris is obsolete. In modern times, we navigate using celestial bodies far closer to home: GPS satellites. Initially, the highest-quality GPS signal was reserved for military use. For security purposes, the American government degraded the civilian signal under a policy known as selective availability. This changed on May 1, 2000, when President Bill Clinton signed a policy directive to provide civilians the same location accuracy afforded to the U.S. military. Even then, however, civilian GPS use was restricted to those who invested in GPS receivers from companies like Garmin, typically drivers as well as avid outdoorsy types willing to invest in a unit to navigate remote backpacking trails. That began to change with the introduction of the iPhone 3G. However, the technological, economic, and cultural implications of the iPhone's first-in-class GPS capabilities weren't immediately obvious. Over time, fewer and fewer people relied on printed MapQuest directions as GPS capabilities became a standard mobile feature. The death of paper navigation was just the beginning of the changes to come.

Global navigation satellite systems (GNSS) like GPS have had so many far-reaching consequences—disrupting entire industries and dramatically changing daily life—that it's become almost impossible to see them. This is especially true for those who came of age after the millennium. GPS is an integral part of the water we're swimming in. When was the last time you were truly lost? When was the last time you hailed a taxi? When was the last time you had trouble meeting up with a friend? We are living in a very different world.

GPS Infrastructure

The companies that build and launch GNSS satellites tend to be stodgy incumbents. In America, Lockheed Martin builds GPS satellites. In other countries, GNSS manufacturers tend to be owned or directly controlled by the government, like China's BeiDou and Russia's GLONASS. One outlier in GPS infrastructure is HawkEye 360,* a private company whose satellite constellation maps radio frequency emissions. Hawkeye 360's "unique ability to identify and geolocate sources of radio frequencies from space reveals previously invisible knowledge about activities around the world," according to the company's website. During the Russia-Ukraine conflict, for example, HawkEye 360's satellites positively confirmed Russian GPS scrambling efforts. Other companies, including Aurora Insight and Xona, are also developing GPS Infrastructure alternatives, ones that are intended to be more accurate, more secure, and more resilient than Lockheed's offering.

GPS Distribution

The GPS Distribution layer mostly comprises companies that have manufactured terminals for decades: Trimble, which introduced the first commercial GPS receiver in 1984, Magellan, Garmin, Qualcomm, and TomTom. However, new entrants are making time and positioning data available to application developers in novel ways. As GPS data becomes increasingly precise and begins to fuse with readings gathered from drones and ground-based sensors, 3D-accurate mapping and positioning will enable a new generation of applications.

For AR to see widespread adoption, we will need back-end solutions that reduce friction and increase ease of use. New York City's echo3D* offers a content management system for developers who are building three-dimensional AR experiences. The company's cloud-based software allows companies to build, store, and deliver these experiences across AR platforms.

The echo3D service allows developers to manage and deliver AR content even in locations with limited bandwidth and high latency. As AR becomes an increasingly popular medium for entertainment, advertising, and other uses, echo3D's platform will be vital to delivering an immersive experience across both satellite and terrestrial data networks.

Tackling another crucial part of delivering immersive AR experiences, Cognitive3D* offers a suite of tools to help application developers track human movement and behavior: where people go, what they do, and even, using eye-tracking software, what they're looking at along the way. For new software applications to deliver on the promise of a fully interactive layer seamlessly integrated into our perception of the real world, this kind of high-fidelity tracking will be essential.

GPS Applications

The GPS Applications layer includes companies that are now household names, such as Uber, DoorDash, and Niantic, maker of Pokémon GO and other location-aware mobile games. It is in this layer that most of the value in GPS has accrued, and the possibilities are still just beginning to be explored. Bliq* and dataplor* are some of the exciting new entrants in the category.

California's dataplor collects and verifies location data for businesses and makes that data available to rideshare companies, food delivery apps, and other applications that require up-to-date information on where everything is.

Bliq, based in Berlin, seeks to improve efficiency on the supply side of the gig economy by aggregating data across platforms. A source of inefficiency in the ride-share and food delivery industries—where even dominant players like DoorDash and Uber struggle with profitability—is all the wasted effort involved in connecting drivers with gigs. For the drivers themselves, finding new opportunities quickly and easily is paramount. Since gigs are spread out across multiple platforms, this requires the use of separate apps that don't talk to each other and just track what's available.

Bliq lets drivers quickly and easily spot the best opportunity in the vicinity, whether that's delivering a pizza for DoorDash or getting a customer to the airport for Lyft. The app uses the location and gig data it gathers to steer drivers toward zones of greatest demand, increasing drivers' profits while boosting network efficiency for the companies that rely on these drivers to serve their customers.

Bliq estimates that 150 million people will be working in the on-demand economy by 2025. Decision-making services like Bliq will play an important role in helping independent workers make the most of their valuable time.

GEOINT

The invasion of Ukraine highlighted the growing capabilities and importance of commercial satellite imaging. As the conflict intensified, GEOINT companies like MAXAR, Planet Labs, and BlackSky provided essential intel not only to world leaders but to civilians worldwide, washing away Russian attempts at propaganda with a steady flow of truth on the ground.

The term Geospatial Intelligence was coined by the National Geospatial-Intelligence Agency (NGA) in 2004 to describe the "exploitation and analysis of imagery and geospatial information to describe, assess, and visually depict physical features and geographically referenced activities on the Earth." Where GPS positions you on the map, GEOINT fills the details of that map in. The global GEOINT market is expected to grow from $63.1 billion to $147.6 billion over the next five years.[2]

GEOINT began as cartography. In Babylonia, maps carved on clay tablets depicted property lines for use in urban planning. The Greeks attempted to map the entire globe, an effort continued and largely completed by European cartographers during the Renaissance.

In the United States, maps contributed to the colonists' victory during the Revolutionary War and the success of the Union Army during the Civil War. But mapping is more than a tool for military planning. In 1854, Dr. John Snow famously mapped survey data to identify the source of a London cholera outbreak, creating modern epidemiology in the process.

Throughout history, higher vantage points have improved our ability to extract useful insights. In 1858, only three decades after the invention of photography, the French photographer Gaspard-Félix Tournachon took the world's first aerial photograph from a balloon over Paris. Eventually, cameras were being mounted on kites, pigeons, and, almost as soon as they had been invented, airplanes. Aircraft, including autonomous drones, still play a crucial role in GEOINT, but only satellites allow for continuous coverage of even the most remote locations. Fused together, GEOINT data from multiple sources and different kinds of sensors can paint an extraordinarily complete and up-to-date picture of any point on Earth.

In 2009, a group of scientists left jobs at NASA and in academia to found Skybox Imaging with the goal of building the first commercial GEOINT satellite constellation. Two years later, Skybox approached Space Capital managing partner Tom Ingersoll to help grow the company. To do that without relying on government contracts, Skybox would need to land big customers in the private sector. As it happened, they were soon approached by one of the biggest of them all.

"Google said to us, 'If you can get imagery of a certain quality, we'll buy all you can get,'" Ingersoll told me. "We asked them for an example image, so they gave us a poster-sized photo of the National Mall in Washington, DC, with the fidelity, contrast, and other factors they wanted. That poster—we called it our Customer Acceptable Image—went up on the wall. Every week, we'd hold a meeting to figure out how close we were to being able to generate an image of that quality."

Having a target to shoot for—pun intended—drove progress. When a Skybox satellite delivered an image that matched the poster's parameters, the business relationship with Google suddenly changed: "'Oh crap,' they realized, 'this is real,'" Tom recalled. Acquisition talks began. In 2014, Google bought Skybox for half a billion dollars. It was the biggest venture-backed exit in the Space Economy up to that point.

"The sale was driven by the quality of the data, the system, and the team we had built," Ingersoll said. "Google wasn't buying a business. They were buying a capability. This is why I always tell entrepreneurs, 'vision without execution is hallucination.' Skybox Imaging sold because we weren't just talking about all this cool stuff you could do. We were doing it. That was the fundamental difference." Today, the Skybox hardware that Google bought, now owned by Planet Labs, continues to send a torrent of high-quality EO imagery to the surface.

A wave of companies followed Skybox. Its approach to building satellites using off-the-shelf components wherever possible represented a dramatic shift from the conventional approach: faster, cheaper, and more effective. Today, innovation in commercial GEOINT continues at a breakneck pace.

The full complexity of GEOINT—comparing the strengths of different sensor technologies, for instance—lies outside the scope of this book. It's also beside the point. In the early days of digital cameras, there was a steady drumbeat of new devices boasting increasingly fine image resolution and other technical improvements. A similar period of rapid progress is underway in GEOINT. Innovation is occurring not only in terms of spatial resolution—how much detail you can squeeze into a single image—but also temporal resolution (how often each area is imaged) and spectral and radiometric resolutions (the kinds of electromagnetic radiation that can be detected by a satellite and with what degree of accuracy).

Each of these areas of innovation offers benefits for certain use cases. But we're still in the early days of GEOINT. The simple but extraordinary feat of photographing the entire surface of the Earth daily, something Planet Labs has been doing for years, is only the start. In fact, collecting data is only part of the GEOINT challenge. Storing and distributing the data generated by all these satellites presents its own difficulties. If you've ever struggled to organize an unwieldy family photo collection, multiply that by the scale of planet Earth and an array of electromagnetic frequencies, and you have some sense of what's involved. Archiving all this data securely and making it easily accessible for software applications is just as crucial a hurdle as building smarter satellites.

Even in 2016, legacy EO vendors like DigitalGlobe, which possessed the largest commercial archive of images at the time, still hadn't adopted cloud computing, meaning all their data remained locked up in on-site servers. (In 2017, GEOINT heavyweight MAXAR purchased DigitalGlobe.) Finding and buying specific satellite images was a difficult, bureaucratic, and expensive process for customers, greatly limiting the potential market.

Long after the digital cloud had transformed other data-driven industries, GEOINT remained a stubborn holdout. To finally open up all that valuable data to smaller customers and new applications, DigitalGlobe used Amazon's "Snowmobile" service to move petabytes—each petabyte is a million gigabytes—of high-resolution imagery from its servers to Amazon Web Services (AWS).[3] Instead of sending all that data to AWS over a normal Internet connection, a process that would have taken months, the data was transferred by cable to special tractor-trailers packed to the brim with hard drives. So much for the "digital superhighway."

GEOINT Infrastructure

Today, a wide array of geospatial sensor platforms are capturing data in different orbits, taking advantage of a new generation of low-cost components and the rise of commoditized storage and computing. The GEOINT's Infrastructure layer includes MAXAR and Planet Labs.

Finland's ICEYE, mentioned in Chapter 1, uses algorithms to identify roads in satellite images and incorporate that data into navigational systems with no human interpretation required. Unlike Planet Labs, which relies on conventional optical sensors, ICEYE uses synthetic aperture radar, which works at night and in any weather.

California's Muon Space* is developing an ambitious satellite constellation to collect specialized scientific measurements for climate change modeling with unprecedented accuracy. It's increasingly clear that insights driven by AI-interpreted satellite imagery will be an essential tool in the fight to mitigate climate change. The climate is a complex and dynamic system and, until recently, climate data has been gathered too inconsistently to create the most useful picture. Muon Space is one of the companies changing that. If we're going to address climate problems head-on, we need to understand them better.

Similarly, Canada's GHGSat* tracks greenhouse gases and other natural and artificial emissions using a combination of satellite- and aircraft-based sensors. The company's algorithms turn this raw data into useful insights for regulatory purposes.

Historically, the energy industry has been slow to adopt monitoring technology that could keep millions of tons of carbon dioxide, methane, and air pollutants out of the atmosphere by identifying gas-mine leaks and other sources of emissions as soon as they happen. GHGSat's cost-effective solution means that both energy companies and regulators can quickly spot and address emission sources.

GEOINT Distribution

Cloud services, artificial intelligence and machine learning, and more powerful APIs and software development kits are bringing GEOINT data into the mainstream by allowing general software developers to weave it into existing workflows. The Distribution layer of the GEOINT stack includes startups like SkyWatch* and Rendered.ai,* along with big data behemoths like Amazon, Google, and Microsoft.

SkyWatch is a Canadian company developing a specialized EO platform to offer fast, easy, and affordable access to geospatial data. By providing application developers with a modern application programming interface (API) to EO data, SkyWatch makes it possible to quickly feed that data into software applications. Space Capital invested in SkyWatch because CEO James Slifierz and his team are finally creating a true marketplace for EO data, removing the barriers to entry for the broader tech ecosystem to use it in valuable new ways. Just as GPS Distribution companies make location data accessible for use in commercial software, companies like SkyWatch will make an array of new GEOINT-based applications possible.

GEOINT data works best when fused together since each type of sensor data offers unique advantages. Rather than mentally assemble a comprehensive understanding of a problem by calling up conventional satellite photos in one place, synthetic aperture radar data in another, and drone footage in yet another, SkyWatch customers can bring all the data from different suppliers together, leading to faster and more useful insights.

One of the challenges of using artificial intelligence to interpret satellite imagery is that any AI needs to be trained with huge quantities of data to improve. Using real satellite data to train AI is both expensive and logistically complex. Rendered.ai, based in Bellevue, Washington, generates procedurally modeled landscapes, vegetation, buildings, water bodies, and cities. This synthetic satellite image data lets data scientists and software engineers build smarter AI for processing real EO images. The data distributed by Rendered.ai isn't genuine, but it provides genuine value in the GEOINT stack.

GEOINT Applications

As an investor, I'm incredibly excited about GEOINT's Applications layer. Though relatively new, this area has enormous untapped potential. Up until recently, EO data was the domain of government, the military, and academia. Now that companies like SkyWatch make it possible for software developers to incorporate this data into everyday applications, the possibilities are endless.

Today, many venture-scale, GEOINT-based businesses are being built in multitrillion-dollar global industries like agriculture, insurance, construction, and financial services. Looking at the market potential on the horizon here, I'm reminded of the rise of location-based services after the introduction of the iPhone 3G. Some of the companies making inroads here are Regrow* and Arbol.* Without question, this layer offers as much world-changing potential as any other in the satellite matrix.

Siddhartha Jha, CEO of New York City's Arbol, hopes to remove the information asymmetry and administrative costs involved in insuring weather-exposed businesses by incorporating state-of-the-art satellite weather data into an insurance marketplace. Extreme weather is a primary source of risk on this planet, and that risk is rising steadily thanks to the growing effect of climate change on sudden weather events like tornados and hurricanes.

One way or another, extreme weather threatens the operations of every business on the planet. Arbol's weather insurance marketplace lets customers in sectors like energy and agriculture transparently insure themselves against verifiable and objective metrics: yearly deviation in rainfall amounts, for example, or extreme temperatures. If an objective metric is met—for instance, if the temperature in a farming region hits a pre-specified high that would damage a certain crop— the insured company automatically receives a payout. With the Arbol marketplace, there is no need to wrangle with insurance adjustors or navigate arcane bureaucratic processes. By increasing efficiency and reducing costs, Arbol can serve millions of smaller businesses previously priced out of the market for this kind of insurance.

As climate change accelerates and the global population continues to rise, precision agriculture will supplement existing tactics like genetic engineering and increased acreage to meet the surging demand for food. Data gathered by GEOINT companies will be essential to ensuring the food supply by helping the agriculture industry adapt to changing conditions more quickly.

The international team of scientists and software developers behind Regrow is based in Australia, which has endured more than its fair share of record-breaking weather events. Regrow uses satellite imagery fused with Internet of things (IoT) sensor data to track crops with unprecedented detail, helping agronomists make better decisions.

For example, Regrow helps farmers in sub-Saharan Africa optimize crop variety and placement based on weather, soil conditions, and other factors, making it possible to maximize output in a challenging agricultural environment. By piping vast amounts of EO and other data into its sophisticated crop models, Regrow makes it easier for the agriculture industry to increase yields even as conditions on the ground continue to defy conventional farming wisdom.

SatCom

It isn't surprising that the first commercial use of space was for broadcasting and telecommunications. On the Earth's surface, sending an electromagnetic signal—a phone call, a radio program—from one place to another is a difficult and expensive engineering challenge. As the distance grows and the terrain varies, successful transmission requires more and more infrastructure while presenting mind-boggling technical challenges. Earth isn't nearly as smooth as it may appear from orbit. All those mountains and valleys have a way of getting in the way of a clear signal, requiring extraordinary amounts of capital investment along with unending maintenance. Even today, large swaths of the population in remote or rural areas are denied the high-speed internet access that is already taken for granted by the rest of us.

All these problems are inescapable down here on the surface. In orbit, the successful transmission of an electromagnetic signal from one satellite to another is all about aim.

Today, the English science fiction author Arthur C. Clarke is best known for award-winning novels such as *Rendezvous with Rama* and for co-writing the screenplay for *2001: A Space Odyssey* with Stanley Kubrick. Clarke is also credited with being the first person to envision the use of geostationary satellites—satellites that stay in a fixed position above a given point on Earth's surface—as signal transmission relays.

"An 'artificial satellite' at the correct distance from the earth," Clarke posited in a 1945 essay,[4] "would make one revolution every 24 hours; i.e., it would remain stationary above the same spot and would be within optical range of nearly half the earth's surface. Three repeater stations, 120 degrees apart in the correct orbit, could give television and microwave coverage to the entire planet." Clarke's essay demonstrated remarkable foresight considering the first rocket to reach orbit had only been launched the year before he wrote it.

As Clarke pointed out, all the technology needed to develop a geostationary satellite already existed back in 1945. However, it wasn't until 1965 that an international consortium actually sent the first such relay into orbit. Intelsat 1, a.k.a. "Early Bird," was the first in a small network of geostationary communication satellites that, in 1969, broadcast the Moon landing across North America and Europe.

If you can position a satellite just over 22,000 miles above mean sea level at the equator, it will travel at the rotational rate of the Earth. Operationally, a geostationary orbit keeps things simple, but it carries a drawback. Twenty-two thousand miles is a significant distance, even for light, creating a small but noticeable delay in the signal. This isn't a problem for one-way satellite TV, but it can introduce an unnerving lag in two-way phone calls. Satellite phone providers like Iridium place their telecommunication relays in LEO. The lower orbit requires each satellite to seamlessly hand calls off to others before passing out of view of the customer, just as cell phone towers hand calls off to other towers as customers drive along the highway. While lower orbits are trickier to manage logistically, they offer satellite phone customers a better way to reach out and touch someone.

SatCom Infrastructure

SatCom infrastructure companies have been around for many decades, but the relatively stodgy incumbents such as Viasat, Iridium, and Luxembourg's SES face new competition in the form of SpaceX's Starlink, OneWeb, and Amazon's Project Kuiper, an envisioned satellite constellation "designed to provide fast, affordable broadband to unserved and underserved communities around the world." (Next, Amazon will just have to figure out how to offer same-day shipping to all those new Prime members.)

Ultimately, SatCom—which has already seen billions of dollars in infrastructure investment and will see many billions more over the next decade—promises ubiquitous, global, high-speed connectivity for all, with applications across the entire tech industry from phone connectivity to IoT to cybersecurity.

SatCom Distribution

The Distribution layer of the SatCom stack is all about gateways, antennas, and terminals: moving data up and down from satellites. The line between Infrastructure and Distribution in this stack can be fuzzy. Some SatCom Infrastructure companies, like Starlink and Amazon, are "full stack," meaning they have or are developing their own Earth-based hardware. The distinction isn't ironclad, however. Starlink has its own ground stations, but Microsoft is also piping Starlink data directly into its Azure cloud. Time will tell which approach to distributing SatCom data makes the most sense for each use case. Other players operating in the distribution layer of SatCom include ALL.SPACE,* Krucial,* and K4 Mobility.*

The British company ALL.SPACE is developing terminals to connect with next-generation satellites regardless of orbit or provider. These universal terminals will offer connectivity out of the box for both terrestrial and satellite-based data networks. Since most existing terminals work with satellites in a single orbit or built by a single provider, it's no surprise that ALL.SPACE has secured multiple military and government contracts for its novel offering. As more SatCom constellations come online, the ability to send and receive data seamlessly across multiple orbits and providers will become essential, just as modern cellphones are now expected to work with different kinds of mobile phone infrastructure around the world.

Even today, as much as 90 percent of the globe lacks reliable cellular connectivity. Remote, uninhabited, and inaccessible areas—including the world's oceans—are peppered with high-stakes infrastructure projects that require continuous monitoring and maintenance. For example, think of the enormous aquaculture farms that help ensure the world's food supply. Scotland's Krucial makes durable, waterproof satellite transmitters that can be paired with oceanographic sensors to automatically send salinity, temperature, and other key measurements to tracking stations located thousands of miles away. Krucial's all-weather, grid-independent, turnkey devices offer resilient, end-to-end satellite data delivery for nearly any tracking purpose. They are increasingly being deployed in mines, on oil fields, at geothermal plants, and near other critical pieces of infrastructure such as railways and other public utilities.

If you rely on a Ring security system to keep an eye on your home while you're away, you understand the value of similar precautions for remote, multibillion-dollar physical installations. Only a few years ago, a train derailed after rounding a bend into an unexpected mudslide in the Scottish Highlands. Laser sensors aimed across the tracks at strategic points paired with Krucial transmitters could have flagged that mudslide long before the accident occurred.

The easier and cheaper it gets for customers to connect to the cloud regardless of their location, the more new use cases open up. K4 Mobility offers an elegant solution for always-on, ubiquitous data connectivity for individuals and IoT devices from cameras to autonomous vehicles. K4's software automatically identifies the best available data networks in range, wireless or satellite, and continuously balances data bandwidth needs against price considerations, all without the need for human intervention.

SatCom Applications

Until now, satellite phones have been so expensive to own and operate that very few people owned them, greatly limiting the market for new applications. As innovation unbundles the SatCom stack over the next few years, the market will grow, and the possibilities will multiply. Themes on the horizon include maritime—recently, Starlink began offering high-speed, low-latency internet access for boats—as well as aviation and autonomous vehicles. It remains to be seen what high-speed internet access anywhere on the planet will one day make possible.

Bringing the Stacks Together

Convergence creates opportunities. One example of convergent innovation is underway at the intersection of GEOINT, GPS, artificial intelligence, and machine learning.

Enormous swaths of land, particularly in less developed nations, still aren't fully mapped. Despite vast quantities of EO data, we still don't have complete and accurate information on every road on the planet, from where each one starts and ends to its current state of repair. Even if human civilization held still long enough that we could bring all the GPS data up to date, the relationship between the map and the 60 million square miles of land it describes would start degrading again as soon as we all resumed scurrying around. Even now, new roads and changes to existing roads can take months or even years to wind their way from the real world into the databases that seek to describe it.

Planet Labs is using algorithms to automatically identify roads from satellite images and incorporate that data into navigation systems without human interpretation. Soon, we'll be able to count on comprehensive and up-to-the-minute maps of every path on Earth. Now that Planet and other companies are increasing the "temporal" resolution of our EO data—the frequency with which each area is imaged—and fusing that with data from drones and ground-based sensors, this approach promises accurate and up-to-the-minute traffic, accident, and visibility data to help drivers operate safely and guide autonomous vehicles. This technology will also help track hazards like storms, floods, eruptions, and earthquakes as they happen.

The coronavirus pandemic highlighted just how fragile the global supply chain has become. Despite extraordinary technological sophistication, all it took was pilot error to completely block the Suez Canal, holding up ships for weeks and exacerbating an already precarious situation. Watching Maersk, the world's largest container line, and its competitors struggle to keep cargo moving from one place to another served as a stark reminder of how modern life depends on mines, farms, and factories an ocean away. If we hope to build resilience back into the supply chain, better information will be key.

Through change detection and remote monitoring for shipping companies, Planet Labs and its competitors help ensure the steady flow of goods around the globe by offering up critical data on demand: How many ships are in port in Los Angeles, and how many are waiting to go in? How many are off the coast of Shanghai today, and are there any notable trends over the last month? This kind of data is gold for shippers—and instrumental for governmental authorities and trade groups tracking everything from piracy to illegal dumping to overfishing.

On land, agricultural companies can gather data on crops and farmland with unprecedented detail, helping them allocate water and fertilizer more efficiently and anticipate crop shortfalls and other issues long before shelves halfway around the world run empty. This is possible not just because of satellites but because we can fuse data from satellites with data from crewed aircraft, drones, and ground-based sensors to create a picture with astonishing clarity.

Combining 3D-accurate location data with computer vision will allow for new applications including highly immersive AR experiences. Though it still sounds like science fiction, AR glasses like Apple's expected realityOS product will integrate layers of virtual imagery into our perception of the real world. If you've observed virtual ads running along stadium walls during televised sporting events over the past few years, you know how seamless this integration can be. The same experience is coming to your personal field of vision sooner than you think.

Yes, this means you can expect customized ads to pop up on nearby walls and other surfaces triggered by proximity through geofencing. Every surface threatens to become a billboard. However, you can also look forward to a sweeping array of handy data at a glance, ranging from heads-up navigation to full-on virtual interactions that take place in your perceived environment. Imagine the kids playing with grandma in the living room even though she's still down in Florida, or an interactive, realistically three-dimensional work meeting at your kitchen table. No more awkward Zoom sessions.

Emerging Industries

Stations, Lunar, Logistics, and Industrials are four Emerging Industries in the Space Economy that have all been covered by the media out of proportion to their actual promise and impact.

Over the past decade, a relatively minor $2.7 billion has been invested across all four. However, while most investment capital in the Space Economy has gone toward satellites and launch, we are beginning to see founders raise capital and build businesses around ambitious new directions ranging from commercial space stations to Lunar transportation services.

There has been one record year after another in the Space Economy, with $46.3 billion invested last year alone across all space technology layers. Infrastructure alone drew $14.5 billion, more than 50 percent greater than the prior record set in 2020. However, much of that capital has chased solutions based on the 10-year-old Falcon 9 launch paradigm. Looking ahead at Starship and beyond, you can see a tremendous amount of opportunity for radically new approaches to building and operating space-based assets.

With Starship expected to come online this year, we are entering a new phase of infrastructure development. Starship promises to be a fully and rapidly reusable transportation system for carrying crew and cargo to Earth orbit as well as the Moon, Mars, and beyond. Able to launch 100 tons inside 1,100 cubic meters for just the cost of fuel, Starship will completely change how we operate in space and enable the four Emerging Industries.

In Chapter 10, I'll take a closer look at Stations, Lunar, Logistics, and Industrials, exploring their surprising potential and clearing up some of the many misconceptions.

***

The point of observing the world through the lens of the Space Economy is as much to notice what's missing as to see what's already here. We're at the cusp of a new S curve of technological innovation and opportunity, and the implications of this inflection point are only just being felt. Hopefully, the gaps you've already spotted in this chapter suggest future opportunities for, among other things, new startups. This leads us to the next chapter, where we will meet some of the Space Economy's most ambitious and ingenious entrepreneurs and gather from them hard-won insights and lessons about building a company of tomorrow.

CHAPTER 3

Chief Orbital Officer: Profiles in Space Economy Entrepreneurship

If you follow commercial space efforts as an industry professional or simply an interested bystander, you may already be familiar with some of the companies and entrepreneurs in this book. Most of us, however, have only glimpsed today's vibrant Space Economy in the mainstream media and remain mostly unaware of the extraordinary progress being made within it. In this chapter, I hope to rectify that.

Without a doubt, business journalists pay more attention to what goes into orbit now than they did five years ago. Even in the technology press, however, SpaceX commands the lion's share of media attention. Part of the reason for this is obvious: A private company is sending customers into space, something that only governments could accomplish a short time ago. Even more noteworthy, the company's ambitions extend all the way to Mars and beyond.

That said, the commercial Launch industry is just the *how* of the Space Economy. More interesting by far is the *what* and the *why*: Now that orbit is accessible to small companies and start-ups, what are brilliant technologists and entrepreneurs worldwide going to do with the opportunity?

Here, I will share fascinating discussions with the founders of an array of exciting companies in the Space Economy, primarily in the Geospatial Intelligence (GEOINT) stack of the Satellites industry. My hope is that seeing the way their services complement each other in surprising and valuable ways will help you understand and appreciate the possibilities in this rich and dynamic ecosystem.

Once we've met some of these key players and learned their stories, we will hear more from them in subsequent chapters when their advice pertains to the specific challenges faced by companies operating in the Space Economy. For now, let's see what they've been working on.

Planet Labs: The Truth About the Planet

Planet Labs, a pillar of the GEOINT stack whose innovative CubeSat miniature satellites revolutionized Earth Observation (EO) in the early 2010s, went public at the end of 2021. Since 2017, Planet's "Dove" satellites have been capturing images of every piece of ground on the Earth's surface on at least a daily basis.

With nearly 500 employees and over 200 advanced imaging satellites in orbit, Planet is a relative behemoth among newcomers in the Space Economy. As discussed earlier, monolithic satellites were the dominant paradigm. Before Planet, one of these satellites—think mainframes in outer space—might give you the opportunity to photograph certain coordinates every couple of weeks. Today, thanks to factors including miniaturization and affordable launch, Planet has blanketed the planet with sensor coverage. Now that temporal resolution—the frequency with which images can be taken—is much higher than ever before, customers can track the surface for incremental changes, a capacity useful for an ever-widening array of applications.

Robbie Schingler is Planet's Chief Strategy Officer. Before founding Planet with fellow NASA alums, Schingler was Chief of Staff to NASA Chief Technologist Bobby Braun. Under Braun, Schingler helped start NASA's Space Technology program.

"I wanted it to be like a venture capital fund," Schingler told me. "You would have different programs across the spectrum of technological readiness. On the low end of the maturity scale, many companies with small budgets. On the high end, a handful that were more mature with larger budgets. That way, you could take risks early on, fail forward, and create a pipeline for technologies that would eventually become operational."

"Sitting on the selection committee, however," Schingler continued, "I felt like I was seeing the same mission concepts from the same players. We just didn't have the ability to get innovation from new people taking different approaches." Frustration with the industry status quo inspired Schingler and his co-founders to enter the private sector themselves. "Dude," Schingler thought to himself, "it's not that hard. It's just an electromechanical device. We can build these things differently."

Before SpaceX, mass constraints had shaped the development of space-based technology more than any other factor. A Space Shuttle launch cost an eye-watering $1.5 billion. Getting a single kilogram into orbit on the Space Shuttle—a liter of water, a toaster, four medium potatoes—cost $54,500.[1] Considering the size and weight of a conventional satellite during this era—as large as a school bus and weighing thousands of kilograms—you begin to understand the thinking behind every design decision. Thanks to SpaceX, however, costs were coming down. Reusable first-stage rockets made access to space several times cheaper per kilogram.

Two other trends created Planet's opportunity beyond lower launch costs: First, the availability of cheaper, more powerful, and more rugged electronic components—radios, batteries, sensors, and so on—driven by consumer electronic device demand. Second, the rise of cloud computing. "As these trends converged," Schingler said, "we thought we could change the economics of space."

In 2011, Schingler and his co-founders left NASA with the goal of building a "planetary utility." This network of EO satellites would accelerate "the sustainability transition of the global economy" by delivering "the truth about the planet." In some ways, Planet's timing was excellent, but as we learned earlier, its founders faced an unexpected "first-mover disadvantage." Satellites aren't of much use if you can't get their data to your customers. Planet had hoped to partner with existing companies in the industry to do just that. However, the founders discovered that getting data down to the surface wouldn't be as simple as renting downtime on someone else's ground stations.

"'Let's see,' they told us. 'This many satellites, this many passes, this many dollars per pass. That'll be 200 million euros a year.'" The pricing models in the GEOINT stack simply hadn't been designed for Planet's use case. The company had to build its own ground stations. "Now, we have forty-eight stations around the world that are bringing down thirty terabytes of data a day," Schingler said. "I'd be happy to decrease my risk by selling them to somebody who can keep upgrading them and making them cheaper. But even today, ground stations are four or five times more expensive than our current costs. So we're still deploying new ones."

Building its own global network of ground stations was only one of several unanticipated hurdles Planet faced in simply getting off the ground.

"To build our first satellite, we needed a radio," Schingler said. "The components available were for university kits: low performance, not useful at all. The smallest S-band radio you could buy was two-thirds the size of our entire satellite and cost half a million dollars." So, just as with the ground stations, Planet had to build what it needed itself.

Problems like these are common for the earliest innovators in any new category. As tough as it can be to overcome them, however, successfully doing so establishes a strong defensive moat: "Building our radio took us two years, but it's our IP, with an amazing radio frequency capability," Schingler said. "There's nothing like it on the market today. What slowed our entry into the market ended up becoming a differentiator."

Today, Planet provides geospatial data for 600 customers in over 40 countries. Its data is used in applications spanning agriculture, government, energy, environmental conservation, and beyond. Planet Labs is now an acknowledged industry leader in commercial EO. "What has helped us maintain our lead is a strong north star," Schingler said. "Having a mission for what we're doing and why we're doing it, and product principles around that mission. Giving yourself a beacon on a hill helps you not get lost as you're tacking, bobbing, and weaving in the art of creation."

Violet Labs: The Right Tool for the Job

Without a doubt, Planet is a major player in the Space Economy. On the other end of the spectrum, many promising startups are rising.

Lucy Hoag is the co-founder and CEO of Violet Labs,* a startup whose cloud-based software makes the hardware engineering process easier and more efficient. We led the seed round for Violet Labs first and foremost because of the quality and experience of its founding team. Hoag and her co-founder, Caitlin Curtis, are engineers with deep experience building spacecraft, launch vehicles, autonomous cars, and drones for companies like SpaceX, Google, Lyft, and Amazon, as well as DARPA. Now, they are improving the tools hardware engineers use across the Space Economy and beyond.

"After building these fantastic, exciting products—honestly, there's nothing better than getting to build a self-driving car—it got to the point where it wasn't fun anymore," Hoag said. "It was so massively inefficient it became painful. So much manual data exchange." Beyond the tedium, frustration, and inefficiency involved in building complex hardware projects the usual way, the process was unnecessarily error-prone: "There's a human in the loop for so many different activities," Hoag said. Hoag and Curtis, who met as colleagues at Amazon, often hypothesized new tools that could make their work fun and exciting again. Though neither had founded a company before, they were tempted by the possibility of building something that might solve all the annoying problems they had experienced as engineers.

"Caitlin and I wanted to build the tool we really wanted," Hoag said, "but we had different perspectives on which solution could solve the problem best." After a "bit of brainstorming," however, the two had an epiphany: "We could build a single tool that addresses the entire hardware development lifecycle from cradle to grave," Hoag said. "A central repository that could bring in data from all the different software tools we were all already using." This approach would sidestep tool fatigue: They knew that the last thing any engineer wants is another piece of software to learn. A tool that consolidated all the data in one place would make things easier, not harder.

Hoag and Curtis wanted to make this tool for themselves. However, they only decided to quit their jobs and launch Violet Labs once they understood the potential market: "These complex, high-margin, multidisciplinary, and often heavily regulated industries are massively underserved," Hoag said. "There are roughly six hundred thousand companies worldwide building complex hardware, from robotics to computers. That number is growing as this type of manufacturing becomes democratized to smaller, newer companies. The total addressable market for what we're building is roughly $50 billion."

Understanding the scope of the market is one thing. Measuring the size of the need at a single company is another: "Tesla, for example, is famous for how much it spends on R&D,"

Hoag said. "Roughly three thousand dollars per car. However, traditional manufacturers like Toyota and Ford invest a good third of that. So a ton of money goes into complex engineering processes. As you'd imagine, automakers invest proportionately in software tools that facilitate these processes. With the diversity of customers we envision, this tool has enormous potential."

Today, the ultimate goal at Violet Labs is to create a cloud-based source of truth for engineering teams across the whole lifecycle of complex products like satellites and launch vehicles: systems engineering and design through supply chain and operations. Just as Zapier and Airtable have become software industry staples by flexibly connecting disparate tools in powerful ways, Hoag hopes that the offering being developed by Violet Labs will become an indispensable part of the hardware engineering workflow in the Space Economy and beyond.

LeoLabs: The View from Below

Violet Labs streamlines the process of building complex hardware for the Space Economy. However, not all this hardware ends up in orbit. Some of the gear with the greatest potential is right here on the ground.

Dan Ceperley is CEO and co-founder of LeoLabs, a company tracking objects in orbit—satellites, spacecraft, and debris—with 10 times the precision of traditional methods for 1 percent of the cost.

"We're building out a worldwide network of ground-based, phased-array radar systems for space traffic management," Ceperley told me. "We have five radar sites so far, with four more under construction, all to keep up with all the new launches and the hundreds of thousands of pieces of debris threatening active satellites. We also build analytical tools that turn this data into risk information about collisions and satellite operations for our customers."

"Our radar network covers all orbits and all inclinations," Ceperley said. "Operating on the ground instead of in orbit gives us unlimited access to electrical power, to computing power, and to communications to get our data into the cloud, letting us scale our network at an unprecedented rate and offer our services at an unprecedented price point." Getting to this level of capability has been an incredible feat for a private startup. "Nobody thought you could do this with a venture-backed company," Ceperley said. "They thought you needed a multibillion-dollar project funded by governments. It provides us with a significant technical moat."

LeoLabs started in 2016, but members of the founding team began developing the underlying intellectual property 25 years ago at SRI International, the storied Bay Area research institution formerly known as the Stanford Research Institute. Funded by the National Science Foundation to do fundamental research on the ionosphere, they had spent years designing special radars to conduct research into upper atmospheric phenomena such as the aurora borealis.

Ceperley, who earned his doctorate in electrical engineering from UC Berkeley, joined SRI later than his future co-founders, in 2008. There, he worked with DARPA and the U.S. Air Force on tracking objects in space. The Air Force wanted to scale this capability quickly to cope with the expected rush of new, smaller satellites driven largely by SpaceX.

Ceperley's work on space traffic management unexpectedly intersected with his colleagues' efforts to study the ionosphere: "Their radars were excellent for ionospheric science but a little too good at detecting satellites and debris," Ceperley said. "For a better look at the Northern Lights, they developed algorithms to identify and exclude that unwanted data. When they heard about my work in satellite tracking, however, they realized that they had unintentionally created what I needed."

Eventually, the three researchers made the decision to leave SRI and bring this new object-tracking technology to market:

"Lower-cost rockets, new, smaller satellites, mega-constellations—it all opened up an opportunity for commercial space situational awareness services. Historically, these services had been a defense activity, but now we could sell to a wave of new customers from satellite operators to insurance companies. We timed it to step out of that research environment just before the inflection point in the market."

"LeoLabs is sort of like the weather service," Ceperley said. "If you're operating a logistics company or a communications company, you need to know about the weather because the weather can affect your business. Now that more businesses rely on space-based assets to operate, they need to know what's going on up there, too."

Fortunately for the founders, SRI International has an active ventures group charged with spinning out new companies. This group incubated LeoLabs and prepared its founders to raise funds and run a business. Spinning out of SRI also made it possible to launch the company with much of the hardware, software, and intellectual property already in place.

"When we started, we already knew that the technical solution was going to be a good one," Ceperley said. "That allowed us to focus on the business aspects from day one. In this way, SRI functioned as an accelerator."

Of course, leaving SRI with valuable intellectual property presented its own challenges: "There's always an internal decision at a research organization about whether to pursue an opportunity as a spin-out or as a more traditional business development opportunity," Ceperley said. "It helped to explain how we were going after a completely different business model, one that required substantial outside investment."

Even after the spinout, the founders had to message the situation clearly to potential investors: "The relationship between LeoLabs and SRI came up often in the early days. We had to show that we were a fully independent company, with SRI as a small stakeholder."

The scope of the growing space traffic challenge boggles the mind: "A few years ago, there were eight hundred active satellites in low-Earth orbit [LEO]," Ceperley said. "Now, there's close to four thousand, soon to be in the tens of thousands. And the amount of space debris dwarfs the number of active satellites. Old satellites, old rocket bodies, fragments of these things. Today, we track debris as small as ten centimeters in size. There are about sixteen thousand such objects in LEO, and another two hundred and fifty thousand pieces as small as two centimeters that are not currently tracked."

Today, building out systems to track smaller debris is the company's primary objective: "If a small piece of debris hits a satellite with enough energy, it can not only destroy that satellite but also generate a fresh cloud of debris, dramatically increasing the risk of operating in LEO. We're building out a network of radars that can track small debris with the necessary accuracy."

This data is also useful for determining best practices for the Satellite industry moving forward: "Our data can show which orbit profiles and satellite constellations are leaving space nice and clean, and which aren't," Ceperley said. "For example, seven hundred and fifty kilometers up is one of the densest altitudes. China destroyed one of its own satellites there, creating a debris cloud, and then a collision between a U.S. commercial satellite and a defunct Russian satellite made things worse. New mega-constellations are going up to 1,100 kilometers, one of the cleanest parts of LEO, and others are going below six hundred kilometers, where defunct satellites and other debris fall out of orbit within a few years—naturally self-cleaning." LeoLabs data will be essential for operators to understand their options and make better choices.

"LEO is much busier now, so active management is even more critical," Ceperley said. "As it turns out, debris causes most of the risk, not active satellites. It's like being on the field during a football half-time show. The active satellites are the marching band, each performer carefully weaving around all the others.

The debris is the drunken fan stumbling onto the field and running into the tuba player."

"Currently, we're serving over 60 percent of the active satellites in LEO," Ceperley said. "In addition to debris tracking and traffic management, we report on satellite health by identifying early signs of malfunction—tumbling, for example, or changes in maneuver pattern. Also, we offer real-time analysis of the risks facing a given satellite or constellation for operators, insurers, regulators, and government agencies."

For any data-driven business in the Space Economy, delivery continues to be a hurdle: "In the past, things in the space industry were bespoke. You had to create specialized interfaces just to work with the data. We're trying to knock that down and become just another layer in the software stack. Every software engineer has programmed with an API, so we send all our information and alerts through one. That gives us reach. We even have a human-readable web page for every satellite and piece of debris in our catalog. On each page, you can see where an object is and every measurement we have on it at that moment."

"The space industry is becoming an important part of the economy as a whole," Ceperley said. "As new commercial constellations come online, these services will become routine parts of the larger business and technology ecosystem. Because of that, it's even more important to understand the place where all these commercial activities are happening. The situation in space directly impacts what's going on down here."

SkyWatch: Bringing the Data Together

Where Infrastructure companies like Planet Labs generate torrents of data, Distribution companies like SkyWatch unlock the value of that data by making it more accessible to developers and their customers. James Slifierz is the founder and CEO of SkyWatch, a company at the forefront of GEOINT Distribution.

SkyWatch provides organizations with the tools they need to integrate remote sensing data into their own applications.

"We believe that EO data should be accessible, affordable, and standardized," Slifierz said. "We do this through two seamless and simple products. The first is EarthCache, which is an API for accessing satellite data targeted at the enterprise. By ignoring the primary market for EO today—government and defense—SkyWatch can tap into all the pent-up demand in the commercial market. We see billions of dollars of opportunity there."

The second core SkyWatch product is TerraStream: "Think of it as 'Shopify for space companies,'" Slifierz said. "It's a solution for operators who need to get their data from a satellite out to customers. Most satellite companies use TerraStream because it helps them easily reach the growing commercial market for EO data."

"Today, we have access to the data from more than 90 percent of all EO satellites in orbit," Slifierz told me. "We also have relationships with more than half of all companies planning to launch satellites over the next couple of years and a contractual relationship with half of those."

Simultaneously, SkyWatch is growing its customer base: "We serve nearly a thousand organizations," Slifierz said, "Just last year, we were serving three hundred and fifty. The year before that, one hundred and fifty. As we figure out how to lower costs even further, we meet more and more customers at price points that allow them to adopt EO data at scale inside their organizations." Companies that have never used EO before are giving it a try because SkyWatch designs its service around their specific needs.

"Whereas it's been standard for satellite operators to require customers to sign a contract and pay a large fee upfront," Slifierz said, "we came to market with a pay-as-you-use model. Customers can start at zero cost and almost immediately use just the data they need. Pay-as-you-use is the way forward, particularly when you're targeting the commercial market. The fact that it's a proven and popular model in that domain is one of the reasons we've seen such good traction in the enterprise market."

Typically, if a company has never previously used EO data, it needs help understanding its full potential. Customer education is an integral part of SkyWatch's value proposition: "We spend a lot of time thinking about where our customers are and the kind of content they might find useful," Slifierz said. "We also position ourselves along the customer journey so that we can jump in and help customers build out their integration, better leverage the data, or simply understand on a deeper level what they're getting and the value it can provide."

Heavy hitters like AWS and Microsoft have entered the Distribution layer of GEOINT, too. SkyWatch, however, sees this as an opportunity to partner: "The big cloud companies recognize the amount of data that's going to be downlinked," Slifierz said, "so they're building downlinking stations at their data centers. This is helpful because one of the most expensive aspects of working with all this data is moving it around. Bandwidth costs can be expensive, especially when you're talking about terabytes or even petabytes of data. The cloud companies are making it easier to get satellite data into data centers."

"We've announced TerraStream partnerships with both AWS and Microsoft," Slfierz said. "The satellite operators that launch using TerraStream as their primary distribution capability will be able to use either AWS Ground Station or Microsoft Azure Orbital to downlink their data directly into the cloud and get it out to customers as quickly as possible."

SkyWatch is also partnering with Esri, an early pioneer in GEOINT. Founded in 1969, Esri was the first company to digitize mapping information for commercial use. "We're running a beta program at the moment with a number of large enterprises that already use Esri," Slifierz said. "They can retrieve imagery directly through the Esri interface without going through SkyWatch. As an API-first company, we want customers bringing EO data into their existing workflows. We don't want them to have a separate workflow for accessing satellite data and yet another workflow to access drone or aerial data. We must be a seamless part of the backend for all of this to work the way we envision it."

To maintain its lead, SkyWatch is investing effort in securing new distribution agreements: "In summer 2022, we rolled out the highest-resolution data available from LEO constellations," Slifierz said. "Images that are thirty centimeters per pixel or sharper. Historically, this level of accuracy has been dominated by Maxar and its WorldView satellites. When WorldView-4 ended its life cycle a couple of years back, Maxar's capacity shrank considerably. Now that a number of startups are promising to launch new high-resolution satellites, we're in talks with every single one of them."

Muon Space: Finding New Ways to See

According to James Slifierz, there are over 280 types of data in demand across SkyWatch's customer base, and only 10 to 15 that are actually available. Where SkyWatch integrates different sets of GEOINT data, Muon Space helps expand the types of data we can gather in the first place. Muon offers companies a turnkey solution for developing custom EO satellite-based sensors. If you need a new kind of EO data for your application but lack the hardware know-how, Muon can help develop a sensor for you and get it into orbit. We invested in Muon's seed round and again in its Series A because they have assembled a truly world-class team and we're excited about the potential of what they're building.

Jonny Dyer is Muon's co-founder and CEO as well as an operating partner at Space Capital. According to Dyer, Muon's vision is focused: "We're not trying to boil the ocean and solve every potential space mission." The company hopes to do for remote sensing what SpaceX is doing for launch by reducing the barrier to entry involved in deploying new sensors.

Central to Muon's approach is a standard data platform for all sensor data: "Everybody reinvents the wheel when they send up a new type of sensor," Dyer told me. With Muon's platform for collecting, organizing, and using sensor data, "much smaller teams can get new sensors up quickly and start building products around that data. There's no need for a bench of rocket scientists and deep pockets just to get to a proof-of-concept."

Addressing climate change is a major use case for these new kinds of EO data. Dyer divides these efforts into two categories: mitigation and adaptation. Mitigation focuses on reducing net carbon in the atmosphere to slow warming in the future. Adaptation, on the other hand, deals with the present. "Even if we're enormously successful at mitigation," Dyer said, "we're going to end up in a world where the climate has changed, and we have to deal with sea level rise, extreme weather, wildfires, and so on." For both mitigation and adaptation, "data is critical."

One adaptation challenge, for example, is larger and more frequent wildfires driven by outdated forest management practices, higher temperatures, and drought. Beyond their effects on human health, wildfires release more carbon into the atmosphere, worsening the climate change that helped cause them. It's a vicious cycle. Muon's EO data allows for more proactive forest management. The company's remote-sensing capability empowers a broad array of organizations and institutions with deep climate expertise but little in the way of satellite skills to get the needed data. This is a perfect example of the power of unbundling in a tech stack. As companies begin specializing in smaller parts of the stack, progress accelerates.

Muon Space and its competitors are benefiting from two complementary trends: more sophisticated sensors and an increase in the quantity of data that can be collected from satellite constellations.

"Getting data down from spacecraft is getting easier because of large deployments of commercial ground station services and because radio technology is very rapidly improving, allowing for very high bandwidths," Dyer said. "The amount of data that can be usefully collected is growing quickly compared with more traditional, NASA-type missions, which often have major data bottlenecks."

A bigger pipe allows for new approaches: "Rather than architect sensors that are narrowly focused on one part of the electromagnetic spectrum, you can have flexible, broadband sensors that vacuum up photons at many different frequencies," Dyer said. "Once you get all that data down to Earth, you can sort through it and build many different applications from a common data set." The flexibility of such "hyper-spectral" sensing allows for a more efficient, multi-mission approach to EO.

The implications of these trends are just beginning to be understood: "When you start thinking about remote sensing in terms of a constellation versus a single sensor," Dyer said, "it fundamentally shifts the way you think about solving problems. Forget 'How do I solve this problem with one exquisite instrument?' Instead, you ask, 'How can I solve this problem with a large array of sensors that, while slightly lower in quality individually, produce much more useful data together?'"

Dan McCleese, Muon's chief scientist and also a co-founder, spent 41 years at the Jet Propulsion Lab, including 10 years as its chief scientist, before entering the private sector. During that time, McCleese had plenty of firsthand experience with the traditional approach to using EO for climate research.

"Imagery still dominates the thinking about climate change," McCleese told me. However, there have been forays into other kinds of observations, some very successful, sponsored by NASA, the National Oceanic and Atmospheric Administration (NOAA), and other agencies. "One such technology that has been commercialized is radio occultation, the use of GPS signals to make enormously precise measurements of Earth's atmosphere," McCleese said. "Radio occultation has greatly improved weather forecasting. It's a prime example of small companies selling EO data to big customers, in this case, across the weather forecasting industry."

"An array of new Earth science data sets are being offered," McCleese said. "Microwave remote sensing of the atmosphere and surface, for example. Making money from these data sets, however, has proven difficult. There are many proposals for data sets that can be commercialized, but the whole industry is in a transition phase." This, of course, is what makes Muon's work so exciting.

"Muon Space is at the forefront of commercializing these kinds of data," McCleese said. "We just need to work backward from the information that can be commercialized to the hardware we'll need to collect it."

Arbol: Risky Business as Usual

More and better EO data from companies like Planet Labs and Muon Space is giving us a whole new level of "truth about the planet," as Planet's Robbie Schingler put it. But what can we actually do with that truth? The industry has only just begun to explore the possibilities. One exciting, near-term application is parametric insurance, which promises to transform how risk is managed across many different industries.

Siddhartha Jha is the founder and CEO of Arbol, a parametric insurance platform founded in 2018. Jha is also a founding partner of dClimate, the world's first transparent, decentralized marketplace for climate data, forecasts, and models.

Applying AI and machine learning to the task of understanding commodities markets at Citadel, Jha experienced the insight that led to Arbol: "Weather is a common threat to nearly all commodities," Jha told me. "These multitrillion-dollar industries all have tremendous swings based on seasonal change, climate change, and weather events like droughts, floods, and heat waves. For example, a heat wave can spike air conditioning demand, forcing a power plant to exceed its budget by buying the additional electricity that it can't generate. Likewise, an unexpected drop in wind speed can cause serious problems for a wind farm. Droughts and floods, meanwhile, affect all crops." Normally, businesses rely on insurance products to mitigate their risks, but the complex and changing nature of weather- and climate-related risks pose unique challenges to the traditional insurance model.

"At the time, you could get subsidized insurance for weather risks," Jha said, "but it didn't kick in until things got really bad. In many situations, farmers were left with large losses despite having insurance. A key function of any market is the transfer of risk, and the insurance market was failing at transferring these climate risks. Meanwhile, the risks were growing as climate patterns shifted. Companies were being hit with climate-caused problems they hadn't had to deal with in the past."

It simply wasn't easy enough for companies to offload weather risks. To Jha, this meant that there was an opportunity in the market. Once he saw that opportunity, he started to think about ways that new technologies and new ways of thinking might fill this market need.

"Arbol started as a white paper on the blockchain space," Jha said. "It proposed using smart contracts to automatically make insurance payouts based on objective data like temperature or wind speed. Certain aspects of the paper aren't yet possible from a regulatory standpoint, but we continue to strive towards the goal of a fully distributed system on the blockchain."

Jha saw objectivity and speed as two critical differentiators for any new approach to insurance. The traditional approach was both too subjective and too slow: "The whole notion of a human loss adjuster subjectively assessing damage from a weather event is a major reason for dissatisfaction with the insurance landscape," Jha said. "When something unexpected happens, as we saw with COVID, you have tens of thousands of lawsuits going around. Is this pandemic covered? How do you assess the damage? Things get delayed, and soon you have clients going bankrupt while waiting for an insurance check."

"The idea behind Arbol was to broaden the adoption of parametric insurance that pays out automatically based on data alone," Jha said. "The biggest parametric use case is climate insurance. Doing this is feasible now thanks to better satellites that can measure things like weather and crop health on a granular level. Previously, it was difficult to confirm that the data applied to the exact spot that had been insured. If you measure weather in a hundred-kilometer-square grid, the actual conditions across a single square can vary greatly at different points. A grape producer who purchased insurance might experience a damaging rainstorm that didn't show up in the overall data for that square. If you can track weather on a one-kilometer-square grid instead, the so-called 'basis risk' is much, much lower."

New satellites provide the necessary level of detail: "You still have weather stations on the ground," Jha said, "but once you leave dense urban areas, forget about it. You need satellite data to fill in the gaps, even in rural America. We have programs in places like Cambodia where the entire country might have one weather station at the main airport. You couldn't do anything like this without today's satellite data."

"The insurance industry had a problem with scale," Jha said. "This inefficiency prevented customers from buying the insurance they needed. At Arbol, instead of sending in human loss adjusters, we rely on objective data from satellites. Instead of recruiting an army of underwriters to handle pricing, an AI engine does it for us. We're bringing the systematic trading approach that transformed Wall Street to the insurance field."

A few years after Arbol launched, dClimate followed as a natural extension: "We had gathered a lot of great climate data," Jha said. "We could have charged exorbitant sums for it as our competitors did. We didn't want to do that. At the time, big companies had been buying up climate data outfits and making that information inaccessible for smaller clients buffeted by climate risk, from municipalities to small businesses. If you wanted hurricane simulation analysis, for example, it could cost 10 million dollars for a subscription. Only the world's largest insurers can afford that. What do you do if you're a municipality prone to frequent hurricanes? Or a small industrial business with a factory in a hurricane zone? The raw weather data might have been freely available, but it was siloed and difficult to navigate. You'd need a team of data scientists to parse it. What's free wasn't user-friendly and what's user-friendly was too expensive."

To solve the problem, Arbol made its data available in a decentralized network: "What dClimate allows the community to do is build analytical tools, visualization tools, forecasts, and other useful things around the data," Jha said. "For example, it now has a tool to estimate how many days of work you might lose due to weather at a given construction site. This had been requested by an insurance broker that deals with construction companies. Previously, there had been no easy way for site managers to assess this risk accurately."

"It's an extremely flexible platform," Jha said. "It can ingest all kinds of data. Today, we're incorporating data around emissions, carbon sequestration, crops, and soil moisture, much of it assessed by satellites. Instead of Arbol hiding its data in a silo, spinning it off as dClimate has allowed the company to leverage the best of what's happening in the climate space. From crop yields to carbon biomass data, dClimate touches on every aspect of the climate. Even in stealth mode, its API gets over a million requests each month, many coming from some of the world's largest commodity companies. That shows the latent need in the market. We haven't even come out with the flagship platform yet. At this point, we would love to have more people using dClimate and seeing how easy it is to get clean weather and climate data compared to the other options out there."

"Arbol itself is dClimate's anchor client," Jha said. "Arbol uses dClimate's data to create parametric insurance contracts. A contract can be as simple as a farmer getting paid because rainfall was below average for the month of July in his area. Or, the parameters can be very complex, such as a blend of wind speed, solar radiance, and temperature to accurately reflect both supply and demand for a renewable energy company. Arbol structures all of this using dClimate data."

"We've seen incredible growth," Jha said, "as well as diversity in our client base: agriculture, of course, but also renewable energy producers, traditional energy companies, and many other parts of the commodities landscape. We're even moving into areas like hospitality. If you rent a house in the Hamptons and it rains every day while you're there, you might get a payout."

"Many novel applications begin as inbound requests," Jha said. "There are many products that would fill a need but are too impractical with traditional insurance methods. Even with all our growth, we're just scratching the surface. A full trillion dollars of crops goes uninsured every year, and there are many opportunities beyond agriculture. The Total Addressable Market is tremendous."

"Our ultimate goal is to build an ecosystem," Jha said. "dClimate lets you analyze your climate risk, and Arbol lets you mitigate that risk. We want to be a one-stop shop for any company that wants to mitigate its climate risk. Every single bank, for example, is being pressured in different jurisdictions to measure their overall climate risk. A loan portfolio of mortgages might have flood risk, hurricane risk, wildfire risk, all sorts of risks sitting in it. Until recently, nobody bothered to quantify any of it. Now, they're starting to, but quantifying the risk to satisfy a regulatory need is only step one. Soon, you'll need to quantify the risk for your investors, stockholders, and board members. Arbol will be there to address that need."

Regrow: Growing More with Less

Arbol and dClimate make it possible for the agricultural industry to transfer the growing risks of climate change. Better EO data also helps farmers adapt their agricultural practices before any insurance payouts become necessary. In the nascent field of precision agriculture, Regrow leads the pack.

Regrow combines EO data with scientific models to help agronomists maximize crop outputs, minimize waste, and mitigate harmful emissions and other agricultural byproducts. Using sensor data from satellites, planes, drones, and ground vehicles, Regrow's analytics engine allows for more precise optimization of irrigation and fertilizer use across vast tracts of land, as well as for the early identification of pests, disease, and other problems before visible signs of distress appear, offering farmers a much better shot at rescuing failing crops.

According to an interview with Regrow's CEO and founder Anastasia Volkova, Regrow is "trying to solve problems around the use of resources in agriculture, making it more resilient, less dependent on fertilizer, and more environmentally friendly."[2] Modern industrial food production is a miracle of scientific accomplishment, staving off hunger for the vast majority of the world's billions, but in terms of greenhouse gas emissions, water and fertilizer waste, and other harmful externalities, twentieth-century farming practices have proven not only economically problematic for food producers but also environmentally catastrophic.

Volkova grew up in Ukraine, where she earned her bachelor's degree in aerospace engineering before completing a master's degree in Poland. Working in various part-time startup roles during her education, Volkova learned "how to attract and retain customers and how to build successful products." Earning her PhD in aeronautical engineering at the University of Sydney in Australia, Volkova worked with an advanced NASA camera system acquired by the Australian government. She quickly grew fascinated with the potential of remote sensing—and frustrated by the limits of the available applications.

"When people think of space, they think of rockets and satellites," Volkova said. "Actually, the most important part of the business model is what you do with the data." With the overwhelming amount of EO imagery being gathered by satellites, it was almost impossible to draw useful insights into what was actually happening on the ground. There was no single source for clear, actionable answers to questions like "Was this grass better than that grass?" or "Is that patch of green wheat or cotton?" The answers are enormously important to preventing soil deterioration, minimizing resource use, and maximizing crop yields, but arriving at them involved mentally integrating many different sets of data.

Living in Australia, where drought is an issue of grave importance, Volkova had a preview of the irrigation issues that will increasingly affect farming across the globe. Meanwhile, she knew that water use management is only one of many areas in which EO data could have an impact. The potential upside was too great to ignore. Still working toward her PhD, Volkova raised $5 million to found FluroSat, which became Regrow.

"We collect all the data from different sources and homogenize it," Volkova told me. "Yield maps, weather sources, farm management software that tells us how the farmer is managing their farm." Using this data, Regrow's software can start answering important questions: Is this crop ahead or behind where it needs to be in its development? Where can we improve its current performance and boost yields? What are the most sustainable practices for this area and crop?

Automatically monitoring a crop using satellite imagery and other sensors, Regrow can alert agronomists when things go wrong and even recommend specific fixes.

"Regrow can give your tractor the map to apply nitrogen," Volkova said. "Or it can tell workers to investigate an anomaly." The AI can even learn: "Once you've applied nitrogen and seen the effects on chlorophyll levels, Regrow will tell you, 'The soil is really fertile, now. Maybe you can get more out of it next time.' Likewise, when a worker scouts out an anomaly and finds evidence of disease, Regrow can automatically identify similar outbreaks across the farm."

Regrow demonstrates the power of sensor fusion, an area with applications everywhere from urban planning to national defense. Where Muon Space allows for more and better sensors to be deployed, companies like Regrow are combining many different types of data to generate actionable insights.

Driving the demand for Regrow is the need to feed a growing world population *without* exacerbating the effects of climate change: "We need to grow more with less," Volkova said. "That's the bottom line, and the technology is now at the point where we can actually start harnessing it." Industrial farms are already highly automated. Tractors, for example, have been autonomous for decades—as Volkova points out, steering a tractor around an empty field is much less complicated than steering a car down a highway.

Today, companies like General Mills, Kellogg's, and Cargill rely on Regrow's data to incentivize more sustainable practices on millions of acres of farmland. The company has raised tens of millions of dollars to fund its expansion to "even more producers and agricultural systems across rangelands, dairy, perennial crops, and more."

In Volkova's view, Regrow's work represents only one part of the enormous opportunity offered by EO: "There's a downstream application for space data in almost every industry."

***

Now that we've met some of the forward-thinking, entrepreneurial innovators leading change in the Space Economy, we can dig deeper into the as-yet-untapped potential that exists across this exciting landscape.

In the next chapter, we will hear more insights and lessons from these leaders as we explore the unique entrepreneurial challenges and opportunities offered by the Space Economy.

CHAPTER 4

No Overhead: How and Why to Start a Business in the Space Economy

For most, the phrase *outer space* still conjures Neil Armstrong, the *Challenger* accident, PBS specials about the Big Bang, and school trips to the planetarium. The idea that someone without aerospace training, an engineering degree, or a military or government background could go raise funding and launch a company that touches on space in some way seems absurd. Or, at least intimidating and unlikely, even for a risk-tolerant entrepreneurial type. Starting a business is tough enough.

Think about it. What's the word for an ambitious effort to do something big? Moonshot.

If you're an entrepreneur with no prior space experience, you may have qualms about entering the Space Economy. Don't let those concerns prevent you from considering all the possibilities. Nobody spots untapped potential better than entrepreneurs, and founders are flooding in, starting space-related businesses in record numbers. All this activity is an indication. There may never be as much wide-open entrepreneurial opportunity again in your lifetime. Consider throwing your hat into orbit.

One Small Step for an Entrepreneur: The Time Is Now

Yes, you need skills, experience, and expertise to start a company—particularly a startup focused on exponential growth—but your background doesn't have to align perfectly to take that first step. Should Larry Page and Sergey Brin have put off founding Google because they hadn't worked at Ask Jeeves for a few years first? Space is new territory for most entrepreneurs, even most technologists. There is too much to be accomplished for every founder to wait until accumulating some arbitrary amount of experience working for, say, a defense contractor.

If you do hail from a space-related background—avionics, satellite communications, defense—you may only know the Space Economy through the other end of the telescope. The typical engineer at a legacy organization like Boeing or Lockheed Martin spends more time on administrative busywork than nuts-and-bolts space tech. From the perspective of someone familiar with those windowless offices and drab cubicles, the idea of starting a business in a WeWork space with a handful of remote peers might seem inconceivable. It's a different world. A venture capital (VC) seed investment wouldn't cover a month of paperclips at a company like Northrop Grumman.

Entrepreneur or engineer, recent grad or career bureaucrat, the Space Economy needs innovative and determined founders willing to try new ideas and aggressively scale the ones that work. Entrepreneurship is the most powerful driver of technological and economic progress, and the Space Economy is an area where rapid progress is currently possible. These amazing possibilities won't be fully realized without many more entrepreneurs shouldering the necessary risks.

Robbie Schingler of Planet Labs sees commercial space as a "new frontier" market, one that "starts from scientific research or government and then, for a variety of reasons—mainly convergence of technologies—opens up a market." In his view, the last such market was the early Web: "I would encourage thinking about the parallels—how the internet actually turned into a global utility," he said.

In Chapter 6, we'll learn more about how and why progress in space stalled between the Apollo missions and the arrival of SpaceX. What's extraordinary about that story isn't why things slowed down as much as how rapidly one company brought decades of stasis to a conclusive end. Even today, SpaceX continues to spur progress across the Space Economy.

As I said in Chapter 1, the Space Economy remains an American-dominated story as of this writing. This makes sense. At its founding, the United States was a bold and intentional experiment in capitalism and self-governance. America is the ultimate nation-startup, and it's been a hotbed of entrepreneurship since its own eighteenth-century IPO. Other countries will keep pace with the United States only to the extent that their governments incentivize and support space-related entrepreneurship within their own borders.

America cultivates entrepreneurs more effectively than any other nation on Earth. No one can say for sure what the Space Economy will look like in a decade, but it will be entrepreneurs, wherever they live, who lead the way as we collectively ascend the S curve of innovation.

Known Unknowns: The Areas of Greatest Potential

During a 2002 news briefing, U.S. Secretary of Defense Donald Rumsfeld infamously contrasted "known knowns" with "known unknowns" and "unknown unknowns" in reference to Iraq's purported stashes of weapons of mass destruction. The Caterpillar from *Alice in Wonderland* might have put the idea a little more clearly. Still, Rumsfeld—whom we'll see again in Chapter 10's discussion of the militarization of space—buried a good point in his statement. There are things we know we don't know. In innovation, these "known unknowns" represent the most direct path to a breakthrough. You can't answer a question you haven't asked.

Certainly, an entrepreneur can tackle a "known known" by offering an incremental improvement on an existing solution. Even then, however, success isn't as simple as building a better mousetrap. If another company provides a solution—launch, for example—you won't break through by doing the same thing they do a *little* faster or a *little* cheaper. Even if you win in a side-by-side comparison, most customers won't bother to switch. Whatever the flaws and inefficiencies of the incumbent, most customers will stick with what they know over the upstart. New offerings rarely live up to their initial promise. Why risk switching providers for the chance at a moderate improvement?

Overcoming inertia requires a genuine level-up, a 10x improvement. At least one key aspect of what you offer—cost, speed, accuracy, and so on—must be so much better in quantitative or qualitative terms that the potential benefits of switching outweigh the real risk you won't deliver.

SpaceX would never have gotten a toehold with a launch service that was 10 percent more efficient or affordable than the Russian alternative. Skepticism about Elon Musk's capacity to deliver on his promises was through the roof from the start. SpaceX had to leapfrog the incumbent with a launch offering that was *far* cheaper and pricing that was *far* more transparent. Even then, the company had a rocky trajectory for years. Giant customers like telecoms can be lucrative, but they are also the hardest to win. If you intend to sell to massive, bureaucratic organizations like defense contractors or government agencies, anticipate the need for a long runway.

The alternative to offering a dramatic improvement over the category leader is to pursue a "known unknown." Professors W. Chan Kim and Renée Mauborgne call this "blue ocean strategy": the search for uncontested market space that lacks an established incumbent.[1]

Seeking out blue ocean in a market isn't about creating a product no one yet wants and convincing people that they should want it. It's about identifying a pressing problem that lacks a robust solution. A known unknown. One of the fundamental allures of the Space Economy is the sheer quantity of known unknowns, the vast sweep of blue ocean entrepreneurs see in every direction.

Lucy Hoag and Caitlin Curtis saw the potential for Violet Labs because, as hardware engineers working at the cutting edge, they were solving their own problem, a problem the market had yet to address. They also knew enough about the industry and their profession to understand that this was no niche product: "Complex products like spacecraft and satellites are no longer the purview of government and big companies," Hoag told me. "The work is being democratized among smaller, more nimble companies, and they all need innovative tools to do their work."

In the Space Economy, there are plenty of known unknowns: technologically feasible things that customers want to be able to do but can't yet with the products and services currently available. As you'll see with many successful entrepreneurs in the Space Economy, noticing an unmet demand like this is often the spark behind the decision to start a company.

A few of the areas currently brimming with potential in the Space Economy include:

- **Next-generation Earth Observation (EO) applications.** Companies like SkyWatch have made vast troves of EO data available through application programming interfaces (APIs). Now that all this data is available to software developers, what will they do with it? From monitoring the supply chain to optimizing shipping routes, how can we use the view from above to generate useful insights about life down here?

- **Sensor fusion.** Satellites offer a persistent, though distant, perspective on any spot on the planet. In exchange for more limited operation time, aerial drones can go in for a closer look. Ground-based sensors, meanwhile, can not only gather imagery but also measure everything from temperature to salinity to radioactivity, all indefinitely, but only from one spot. Sensor fusion brings these complementary perspectives together for greater insights. In agriculture, combining data from the many different sensors already on a farm is transformative. As Regrow founder Anna Volkova told me, "Tractors have been autonomous for decades—a satellite tells the tractor where it is and where it needs to go. Meanwhile, you have sensors measuring soil moisture, the flow rate in your tanks. Even the cows' ear tags are connected." Where else might we leverage fusion? What about a marketplace for drone data? If a mining company wanted a close-up look at an interesting, remote geographical feature on a satellite image, it could post a request and get live footage taken by a local drone hobbyist. The possibilities are all around us.

- **Augmented Reality (AR) applications.** Niantic's Pokémon GO is just one app that leverages user location data to offer a customized experience. Startups are experimenting with everything from targeted ads that only appear when you're within walking distance of a particular retail store to smart home features that activate when you approach your house.

- **3D data and development tools.** If you've used Google Earth before, you've seen the progress Google has made in transforming two-dimensional satellite images into roughly accurate three-dimensional environments. That's just the beginning. More sophisticated digital tools will allow developers to arrange, manipulate, and otherwise process geospatial data in valuable new ways.

- **GPS alternatives.** GPS is vulnerable to jamming and other malicious attacks. Also, it isn't accurate at the meter level. Other methods of positioning and navigation will complement and enhance GPS, allowing for meter-level accuracy even in areas where a strong GPS signal is hard to acquire. Newer methods will also add resiliency to this crucial piece of infrastructure. There are several promising avenues being explored here, including using Earth's magnetic field.

- **Ocean observation.** The oceans, which cover 70 percent of the surface, are too large to monitor comprehensively using traditional methods. HawkEye 360 uses its satellites to locate ships that have deactivated their beacons. Regulators use this data to send drones in for a closer look, helping identify pirates, smuggling vessels, and illegal fishing operations. Moving forward, algorithms will spot patterns in satellite images without human intervention, useful for regulatory purposes and providing valuable intel to the shipping, fishing, and aquaculture industries. There is also potential in Satellite Communications (SatCom) smart buoys that collect and transmit oceanographic data in real-time or signal nearby vessels to avoid colliding with fishing nets, a problem in ocean fisheries around the world.

- **Weather micro-forecasting.** Though modern weather forecasting is well over a century old, it is still a developing science. Meteorologists continue to struggle with macro predictions over short timeframes. Unfortunately, faster supercomputers and smarter algorithms can only do so much to improve accuracy when most of our weather-sensing infrastructure hasn't been upgraded in decades. Weather can be highly localized. We need more and better data now, particularly about microclimates like the famously cool and moist zone in the San Francisco bay area. You need granular data to make useful predictions. Tomorrow.io provides action-able weather insights to companies ranging from Delta and United to the NFL and National Grid, helping them manage the impact of weather on their flights, football games, and power grids. There are many other potential customers in this space. For example, farmers of high-value crops like almonds and wine grapes will likely buy accurate weather forecasts about very small areas. Doing this will require new weather sensors and software with a microclimate focus.

Some parts of the Satellites Industry matrix—GPS Infrastructure, for example—boast a rich array of incumbents and upstarts. Others, like SatCom Applications, remain wide open. The matrix is useful partly because it highlights the areas where existing technological capabilities are only lightly explored. Center your thinking on each part of the matrix and consider what might be possible given your expertise, experience, and entrepreneurial inclination.

"The area I really like is Infrastructure," Dan Ceperley of Leo-Labs told me. "There's a gold rush going on. LeoLabs is supplying information to space companies with a very healthy future in front of them. Pay attention to the ones providing foundational services that other companies will build on top of, like launch operators, space situational awareness companies, and satellite operators. The industry is moving from vertically integrated to having all sorts of different service providers, and the shift will make the innovation cycle go even faster. We're going to see winners in the satellite constellation arena, but we're also going to see winners in many supporting services and technologies."

"This is a once-in-a-lifetime opportunity in the space industry," Ceperley said. "Whether you're investing, launching a new company, or working on some new technology, it's a great time to jump in. The price of accessing and using space is going down, and you can rely on modern computing technologies to do things at a much larger scale."

Space Economy Jobs as Entrepreneurial Launchpads

Instead of seeking out problems systematically as described previously, many entrepreneurs stumble onto their ideas in the course of their daily work. This is why curiosity is so important. Become willing to stop in your tracks when you notice something unusual or unexpected—a small problem can sometimes become a big business.

Many startups spring up from within the industries they eventually disrupt. Entrepreneurial employees naturally want to fix the problems they encounter, and large organizations rarely have much appetite for disrupting their own business models with something new. While big companies can be good at incremental improvement, when it comes to what's next, start-ups take the lead.

If you already work in or adjacent to the Space Economy, your first and most important task as an aspiring entrepreneur is to keep your eyes open to the unsolved problems around you. Don't seek out the "perfect" idea to pursue. Instead, keep a list of new ones as they crop up and make a habit of exploring them. Above all, seek to confirm the market for any given idea. Solving neat problems is fun, but is this something that somebody, somewhere, would conceivably pay for?

After earning his master's in electrical engineering and a PhD in physics from Duke, Rendered.ai CEO and founder Nathan Kundtz went to work at Intellectual Ventures, a Bellevue, Washington-based private equity firm that develops and licenses technological patents.

Kundtz's position gave him the rare opportunity to work closely with an array of scientists and engineers developing new products based on cutting-edge technologies. When Intellectual Ventures spun out a company called Kymeta, which was based on a new antenna ideal for SatCom applications, Kundtz became its CTO and eventually its CEO.

When Kundtz subsequently founded Rendered.ai in 2019 to develop synthetic sensor data for training and validating artificial intelligence software, Kundtz was already familiar with every stage of founding a business. Between the world-class technical education, the first-hand exposure to real-world innovation, and the leadership roles in tech companies, it's hard to imagine a resume more ideally suited to a Space Economy entrepreneur than the one Kundtz assembled.

Kundtz's story is an excellent example of how exposure to real-world industry problems spurs valuable startup ideas. Working in the Satellites industry, he had the opportunity to observe the challenges facing application developers who were training AI to interpret vast amounts of data.

"Artificial intelligence algorithms are ultimately driven by the data used to train them," Kundtz told me. "Recently, the government said they need 50 million images for every object they're trying to identify to achieve 60-percent-accurate detection. That becomes very expensive when you think about data collection as well as annotation: having humans come in and tell a computer what's in each image. Also, you still miss rare events and edge cases doing it this way, which is incredibly important to algorithm performance. Eighty percent of the time and expense invested in building these algorithms is dedicated to getting access to data sets."

These observations sparked the idea of generating artificial data for AI training purposes. This led Kundtz to found Rendered.ai. If he hadn't known that AI training had become an expensive hurdle for application developers, it's unlikely he would have stumbled on this idea another way. As it turned out, synthetic image data has applications across the entire area of AI image analysis, useful everywhere from autonomous driving to medical scanning to weather forecasting.

None of this means that you need a robust industry background to consider founding a company in the Space Economy. Just think carefully about the unique skills and experiences you bring to the table as an entrepreneur, and figure out an approach that will make the best use of them. Know your strengths and lead with them.

The full art of entrepreneurial innovation lies outside the scope of this book. Still, there is no question that you will need to explore different ideas before you zero in on something with the potential to attract investors. Stay flexible and open, even if you feel like you're onto something valuable and urgent. You may need to pivot repeatedly as you feel your way forward to a problem customers will pay you to solve.

This assumes you have at least some exposure to the Space Economy. If you aren't even adjacent to businesses that fall within its scope, start by doing your homework. In the Introduction, I talked about my experience helping Astrobotic develop a market assessment for commercial lunar transportation services. I didn't find that opportunity posted on LinkedIn. I dreamed it up myself and pitched it to the company because I wanted the first-hand experience they could offer. Astrobotic agreed because they would benefit from what I brought to the table.

To succeed as an entrepreneur in the Space Economy, you need some familiarity with it. When you're just starting out, that means either securing the right job or volunteering your services to get your foot in the door as I did. Luckily, it's much easier to gather that valuable experience today. There are more commercial space companies than ever before, and like any other organization, they need everything from bookkeeping and HR support to online marketing and financial reporting. The advantage of continuing your "old" career as the first step to entrepreneurship is the "all hands on deck" culture in a startup. If you bring your hard-earned career skills to the table, you may not get to design a satellite on your first day, but you'll discover opportunities to contribute in areas outside your core responsibilities, build experience and learning skills, and spot opportunities along the way.

There's no substitute for time in the trenches. I count my experience at Astrobotic as formative, and I encourage entrepreneurs who lack industry experience to do as I did. Get a job that fits your skill set within the Space Economy. If you don't see it posted on the job boards, pitch it instead.

Whatever you do, don't fall for Silicon Valley's breathless hype about college dropouts building the future in their garages. Nobody sees more entrepreneurs on their way up than someone in my position, and I can tell you that they all come to the table with some amount of experience and expertise. They know the territory and they have skills, even if the road ahead poses unfamiliar challenges. The brilliant newbie turned industry titan is pure media myth-making. Even if you have no long-term interest in a conventional career in the Space Economy, one of the tested paths to successful entrepreneurship in any industry has always been to spend time as an employee within that industry.

Job experience will expose you to the known unknowns. It will also offer lessons in everything from hiring and managing to marketing and selling, all while earning a salary. An MBA can be useful, but nothing will teach you the fundamentals of running a business faster than watching somebody else fail at the basics. Once you feel confident you can handle a business better than your boss, go prove it.

If this path to entrepreneurship appeals to you, Chapter 8 will tell you how to build a career in the Space Economy, from establishing a professional network to working your way up the ladder. When you consider the fact that nearly every successful entrepreneur in tech started out with related career experience, this approach seems like the safest bet.

As a group, of course, aspiring entrepreneurs are not known for their patience. With the Space Economy making news daily, it may feel unbearable to consider spending years working on someone else's dream during a period of such extraordinary growth and opportunity. If that's true for you, there are still things you can do to mitigate the risks of entrepreneurship and maximize your odds of success.

Learning the Landscape

Forget the idea of mission control rooms with giant screens and rows of flashing buttons. Most of the real work in the Space Economy takes place at a laptop or around a conference table. Outside of the Infrastructure layer, your workspace probably won't be situated next to a giant hangar or launch site either. If anything, remote work is even more prevalent in the Space Economy than elsewhere.

As a founder, there's no need to look like John Glenn or Neil Armstrong, either. While there are real diversity hurdles to be overcome—just as in the tech industry as a whole—the "right stuff" in the Space Economy has very little to do with the college you attended, let alone your native language, accent, or the color of your skin.

One exciting aspect of any new market is the potential for social mobility. In 1996, no one could claim five generations of distinguished web developers in their family lineage. If you haven't felt welcome in other industries for whatever reason, know that the Space Economy is relatively open and inclusive.

Outer space is highly regulated but, like any area of white-hot innovation, those regulations can't keep pace with the rate of technological change. As we've seen with industry disruptors like Uber, one of the keys to scale is figuring out where the regulations are fuzzy and then pushing hard and fast on those areas before regulatory bodies, trade groups, industry watchdogs, and other elements formulate an effective defense. (Of course, it's possible to push too long and too hard, with serious consequences, also as seen with Uber.)

Disrupting a highly regulated environment requires staying abreast of the landscape. In the case of LeoLabs and space domain awareness, the U.S. Department of Defense was already providing tracking and collision-warning services: "If a piece of large debris was likely to go close to a satellite within the next week or so, they would send out a notice," founder Dan Ceperley told me. "In 2009, when there was a large collision between a

U.S. commercial satellite and a defunct Russian satellite, the U.S. government was probably the only organization in the world with the sensors and services to identify potential collisions."

It's hard to compete with free. However, with the number of satellites increasing exponentially, the Department of Defense was looking to leave the space traffic management business altogether. LeoLabs seized the opportunity: "We are taking the load, with over 60 percent of all active satellites in LEO using our collision avoidance service," Ceperley said. "Nobody else has developed the scalable architecture necessary to address this."

Government agencies operate very differently than private companies. For startups, these agencies can be customers, competitors, or both. As an entrepreneur in the Space Economy, you must navigate this with "legislative finesse," according to Dan McCleese of Muon Space. "It's hard to break in," he told me. "Many commercial data sets fail to find footing because government agencies and other organizations already offer similar sets for free." The National Oceanic and Atmospheric Association (NOAA), for example, makes its weather-forecasting information available for general use. If you're looking to develop your own meteorological sensor, for example, the question becomes, what data is still needed in the commercial market that is also technologically feasible to collect?

The advantage of a private company is that it can go precisely where the opportunity is without sweating larger administrative priorities. "NASA," McCleese said, "chooses to address climate indicators in each of the major categories such as ocean science, land, or atmosphere. In doing so, it sprinkles money around. Support does go to good science, but it's challenging to say, '*This* must be next.'" In contrast, industry faces no such requirement. Instead, companies can focus on the "fuzzy" question of who the user might be, who might ultimately pay for the data.

"Let's say you had a silver-bullet climate measurement," McCleese said. "Who are the users? Is the modeling community prepared to begin paying for data, which they largely don't do now? If so, where will they get the funds to do that? Oil and gas is one area where the demand for commercial data appears to be real. Clearly, there are resources there to fund data capture and analysis. In natural gas, EO data drives cost savings. If a gas company can identify a methane leak, for example, it can recover money by fixing it. The same is true for the plastics industry, where there are regulation-driven constraints on manufacturing emissions and more regulatory limits likely to come. Now there's some motivation for data purchasing."

If you want to break in, adopt McCleese's way of thinking. To succeed as an entrepreneur in the Space Economy, according to Muon's Jonny Dyer, it's crucial to "understand the interaction of commercial market forces and government policy and regulation." Ignore the larger landscape at your peril.

The Ground Is Constantly Changing

We're exiting the Wild West stage of the Space Economy. Regulations are tightening up. As you recall, chaos once reigned in ride-sharing, much to the benefit of rule-flouting Uber. Now that Uber is dominant, the regulatory environment is much more strict. Space is following the same pattern.

There's a positive side to intense government scrutiny. As private companies widen the horizon of possibilities, more government money becomes available to fund promising ideas. In fact, government is where many entrepreneurs get the first dollars they need to create the prototypes necessary to pitch private investors, as we'll see in the next chapter.

For all the libertarian spin around commercial spaceflight and the myth-making around Elon Musk, Musk himself was happy to admit the importance of government support in getting SpaceX off the ground.

"I would like to start off by saying what a tremendous honor it has been to work with NASA," Musk said at a 2012 press conference after the successful launch of SpaceX's Dragon capsule, "and to acknowledge the fact that we could not have started SpaceX, nor could we have reached this point, without the help of NASA."[2] In its first decade, SpaceX depended heavily on progress payments on NASA contracts to continue its operations. SpaceX, like many other companies in the Space Economy, is the fruit of a public-private partnership, a collaboration between business and government. This model will remain important well into the future.

***

The Space Economy offers the aspiring entrepreneur world-shaking potential in any direction you might look. You'll find no desperate picking over of small ideas and minor improvements here. Startups are chasing huge, impactful outcomes that, if successful, will improve life on this planet for millions and even billions of people.

This is why the most talented people in the world are turning away from opportunities in lucrative areas like investment banking and consumer software to join our ranks. World-class talent responds to a challenge. There are few challenges as invigorating as ones like mitigating climate change, feeding the hungry billions in developing nations, or giving people trapped in repressive regimes internet access.

"I really wanted to make a sustainable impact," Regrow's Anna Volkova told me. "I wanted to look into the eyes of my kids and say, 'Mom has done something to make the world more sustainable so that you can live in it and your kids can live in it.' When people think of rocket scientists, they think we dream about going to Mars. Regrow might one day have a module for growing potatoes there, but my vision is to fix what's happening here first."

In 1968, Apollo 8 sent back the legendary "Earthrise" photo of Earth taken from the Moon. This powerful image helped spark the environmental movement. What we do in outer space profoundly matters to humanity in ways that many other lucrative commercial activities do not. Think about this as you consider where to direct your own entrepreneurial ambitions.

If starting a company in the Space Economy appeals to you, you're probably wondering where to begin. In the next chapter, we'll take a look at what it takes to succeed as an entrepreneur here, where to start your journey, and what to do once your company is off the ground.

CHAPTER 5

Charting a Trajectory: Co-founders, Customers, and Capital

The founders we invest in typically aren't ready to scale up just yet. Most still need to find product-market fit. At the seed stage, entrepreneurs use investment dollars to hone their offerings to zero in on what customers will actually buy.

In the previous chapter, we looked at areas of potential in the Space Economy, as well as some of the ways aspiring entrepreneurs discover promising business ideas. Moving from a general solution to a viable business begins with identifying the right market for that solution. Once you know who your first customers might be, it's your job to learn more about them and their needs.

Forget "nice to haves." Businesses are built on "need to haves."

Start with the Customer in Mind

"'Who is the customer?' is the first and the crucial question in defining business purpose and business mission," wrote management expert Peter Drucker.[1] Knowing whom you plan to sell to won't do any good, however, if you've never spoken to those potential customers. To get the answers you will need to proceed—from the features they want to the prices they are willing to pay—the only approach is to go ask.

"Before Arbol, weather risk insurance was stuck in a chicken-and-egg scenario," founder Siddhartha Jha told me. "When a market is small, few want to put capital in. A small market is risky, illiquid, overly concentrated. The weather risk market was basically a few pockets of risk in certain parts of the U.S. and Europe—not great in terms of diversification. Worse, since the insurer is shouldering all this risk, it has to charge a high price. When insurance is too expensive, you don't get repeat business."

"To break that feedback loop," Jha continued, "we did the tedious work of simply talking with many different types of clients in order to fully understand what they needed. This is something that nobody had bothered to do, especially in the farming space. Those conversations made it clear that many different companies needed something similar and nobody was providing it. There was enough unmet need to get the capital side interested."

Even if you have a general idea of what you will provide, the "tedious work" of early customer conversations will guide you toward product-market fit. You'll know you've found that fit when the entrepreneurial process—from generating leads to raising capital—becomes suddenly easier. If you've landed on something people really want, things take on a certain momentum. Instead of pushing a tepid idea uphill, pivot to one that generates excitement in every customer conversation.

Don't overcomplicate this process. Look for the straightest possible line from A to B. Lucy Hoag and Caitlin Curtis of Violet

Labs reached out to their professional networks as a first step: "Caitlin and I have been at it in our careers for a while," Hoag told me. "We feel pretty fortunate to have really great networks, a lot of people we respect both in established companies and in the startup world. We used that for our first round of outreach, being those annoying people asking all their friends for a favor." At the time, former colleagues of the two founders were leading product teams at companies like Rocket Lab, making them ideal for initial outreach for the startup's cloud-based engineering workflow tool.

Hoag and Curtis knew that being able to reach someone in the right position was only half the battle: "Caitlin and I were diligent about organizing our pitches over time," Hoag said. "We were also thoughtful and deliberate about whom we approached. At the beginning, we talked to a few dozen potential customers across a number of industries. Aerospace and defense, self-driving trucks, robotics, medical devices, consumer electronics, even personal fitness and wearables. Generally, we got over-whelmingly positive feedback. 'Could you build this yesterday?' they asked us. 'We really need this now.' The frustration was tangible."

These initial, successful conversations were the first domino: "The more people we talked to and shared our deck with and talked about the problem with," Hoag said, "the larger we realized the market could be. We had people we didn't know reaching out to us on LinkedIn, even texting us. It became an organic process. When you have something the market wants, word spreads, and now we've been fortunate to get into new industries outside of aerospace: robotics, medical devices, automotive, agriculture." That's product-market fit in action.

Looking back at the company's successful seed round, Hoag calls it "bonkers" how easy the process was: "I don't say this to toot our own horns," Hoag said, "but as a testament to how badly this product is needed. It resonated really strongly with so many folks. So yeah, we were pleasantly surprised."

Even after you've found product-market fit and gotten your company off the ground, you can never afford to stop talking to customers. At Muon Space, for example, every mission begins with a customer need. The goal isn't to deploy every kind of satellite-based sensor imaginable in a "build it and they will come" mentality. Instead, Muon dives deeply into the nature of the problem and develops a remote-sensing solution that is ideally suited to solving it before launching a single satellite.

"We're engaging with customers in these markets early," Muon CEO and co-founder Jonny Dyer told me. "This happens long before we even have the idea of an engineering solution for a sensor." Partnering with its customers from the start, Muon works "from an early idea through having data streaming into a cloud bucket in their organization."

Prioritizing the customer's needs this way differentiates Muon in an increasingly crowded niche: "We're not trying to sell a data set that we happened to collect and are hoping somebody will buy," Dyer said. "We want to collect data that is absolutely crucial to the problem that our customers are trying to solve. The depth of experience we bring on both the engineering and the science of remote sensing puts us in a unique spot to do that."

"Be maniacally focused on your customers," Planet Labs co-founder and Chief Strategy Officer Robbie Schingler told me, echoing Dyer. "It's critical to get the voice of the customer from the very beginning. You're solving a problem. Focus as hard as you can on a particular, vertical market." Of course, this raises the question of which vertical market to focus on—a single technological solution might have applications across a broad range of industries. You have to begin somewhere, but choose wisely—your first customers will inevitably shape the trajectory of your business.

Unlike many startups in the Space Economy, Planet Labs began not with government agencies but with the agricultural industry instead: "Your earliest customers influence you the most," Schingler said. "Choose ones who are pragmatic about what they need from you today and also understand that you are building a differentiating capability for them and their business over the years. You want customers who are willing to go with you on that journey."

By listening to the right customers early, "you build for someone in particular, not just yourself," Schingler said. "Listening doesn't mean you always do what they say. But you earn trust with your early adopters by doing what you say you're going to do and always having the voice of the customer inside your walls. That's necessary to build a product that satisfies the user's needs. It also pulls you into the future rather than holding you back. If you have high integrity with your customers and build a long-term partnership, they'll be willing to bet on you to keep disrupting yourself in order to advance their mission."

Like Planet Labs, SkyWatch takes a strategic, long-term approach to its customer focus. "While more than 90 percent of EO [Earth Observation] revenue in general comes from government sources," SkyWatch's James Slifierz told me, "government sources account for less than 5 percent of Sky-Watch's revenue. That's because of our commercial focus. We're here to democratize satellite imagery. Our end goal is for EO data to have the same power and impact on the world that GPS data has had over the last two decades."

The commercial market for EO works differently, so this focus is important to steering SkyWatch's growth: "Government buys large amounts of data at a time: imagery of cities, counties, states, even countries," Slifierz said. "However, aside from natural disasters and military conflicts, it doesn't need this imagery on a very frequent basis." Commercial customers, on the other hand, require imagery of smaller areas, but on a much more regular schedule. "You might want to monitor a construction site on a weekly basis," Slifierz said. "A farm, every three or four days. Previously, the cost structures of EO haven't supported these commercial use cases. By automating the entire process from ordering to delivery, we've made EO data more efficient and therefore more affordable for ordinary businesses. Accessing satellite imagery should be as seamless as watching Netflix. We're succeeding because we've done a really good job of understanding our market, segmenting that market, and building a customer success program that helps specific groups make the most of EO in different contexts."

In any area at the edge of technological innovation, studying customer usage data is essential to identifying and validating demand for new products: "We have access to an amazing amount of market intelligence, not only from the millions of API calls we have on our platform but also the data we capture in our customer conversations. Our upcoming product, tentatively called EarthCache-X, allows customers to get the data they need even if we haven't integrated it yet. This saves them time while allowing us to validate the demand for that data set. For something cutting-edge—a new hyperspectral capability, synthetic-aperture radar, something interesting with LIDAR— EarthCache-X lets us measure the market demand."

The business you are building may change in fundamental ways several times as you orient yourself toward product-market fit. That's why the right management team can be even more important than the specific offering you think you want to provide. The road to the winning product or service is rarely straight. For us, a resourceful team of founders with resilience, experience, and expertise is worth more than any single business idea. Choose your co-founders as carefully as you do your customers.

The Well-equipped Founding Team

What makes for the perfect founding team? Most important, of course, is that it's never one thing. (If a venture capitalist figured out the formula for a great founder, they'd leave the rest of us in the dust.) Journalists tend to highlight a glamorous subset of success stories, but effective founders come in all forms. Their backgrounds and personalities are far more varied than you might expect from the fawning media coverage. There are, however, common elements.

The first is grit. When founders pitch us, we look for the willingness to keep trying different things until something clicks. The second is flexibility, an openness to input. If you go into every conversation convinced that you're completely right about everything you think, you won't go far. Even Steve Jobs listened to experts before making the call. He was just better than most people at deciding which experts to ask—and when to follow his gut in the face of that advice. In most cases, Jobs knew enough to know what he didn't know.

A successful founding team is all about complementarity. Working on Project Kuiper, Amazon's broadband internet constellation, Hoag met her future Violet Labs co-founder.

"Caitlin and I have pretty interesting vantage points on the product development lifecycle," Hoag said. "My career has mostly been on the first half: system engineering, requirements, design analysis, integration, and testing. Caitlin, roughly speaking, the second half: manufacturing, operations, dealing with supply chain issues. It was a really natural fit." Hoag and Curtis bonded over their shared frustration with the modern process of complex product development, something they were both intimately familiar with from a breadth of different experiences at world-class organizations.

After his first experience in the Space Economy at Skybox, Jonny Dyer became an advisor at MethaneSAT, a subsidiary of the nonprofit Environmental Defense Fund that uses satellites to track methane emissions. Methane is an especially potent greenhouse gas thought to be responsible for a substantial proportion of global temperature increases. Advising MethaneSAT, Dyer connected with future Muon Space co-founders Dan McCleese and Reuben Rohrschneider.

For entrepreneurs, mission-driven positions, including volunteer roles, are an effective way to build their professional network while connecting with potential allies. Advising MethaneSAT, Dyer, McCleese, and Rohrschneider realized there were other measurements beyond methane levels that might be useful in the fight against climate change: "MethaneSAT is great, but it's focused on measuring methane emissions going into the atmosphere," Dyer said. "Brainstorming, you can come up with thirty additional measurements that will be critical to mitigating and adapting to climate change in the future."

The chance to do well by doing good catalyzed the founding of Muon Space. If they hadn't volunteered to help MethaneSAT, Dyer and his co-founders might never have considered the possibility of starting the company—or found the right partners to do so.

Setting Yourself Up in the Right Place for Success

When asked why he robbed banks, Willie Sutton famously replied, "Because that's where the money is." Even in the era of remote work, geography remains an important factor. In many cases, you can base your operation right where you are now. However, there was a good reason Elon Musk based SpaceX in Los Angeles: That's where the rocket engineers were. Likewise, Musk based Starlink in Redmond, Washington, a short distance from Seattle, to leverage the concentration of software talent in the area.

Building a great team, finding potential customers, and pitching investors are all tasks that can be made easier or harder depending on where you plant your stake. Location is important, particularly in the Space Economy. Before you settle on one, ask yourself: How might this location hold us back, and how might another help us succeed?

Specialized talent is one of several factors in deciding where to position your startup. If you need plenty of on-site engineering talent, bite the bullet and make the move to a tech hub instead of spinning your wheels in the hinterland. State and local taxes, regulations, and government incentives can also be significant considerations depending on the nature of your envisioned business. If scaling up your idea would involve hiring large numbers of employees, then factors like local wages, cost of living, and even crime stats and school quality will matter. (More on hiring in Chapter 9.)

Consider one final factor in regard to location. Operating in the Infrastructure layer of the Space Economy often requires access to launch services. All things being equal, if you're going to be manufacturing anything intended for orbit, you may want to base at least part of your operation near a launch pad. SpaceX has facilities at Cape Canaveral, among other places, because of the existing launch infrastructure that is already there. That infrastructure is already there because Cape Canaveral is as close to the equator as you can get in the continental United States while still being able to launch over water. Companies change, but geography stays the same.

Harnessing Government Support

In this industry, you'll need to cultivate or hire the ability to sniff out pots of government money. At Space Capital, we often write the first institutional check a founder receives, but even at that stage we expect some traction, and finding traction costs money.

We don't see much value in incubator programs for this purpose—incubators typically ask too much of founders for too little in return. In the Space Economy, the government makes for a much better source of the earliest funding. Regardless of your home country, educate yourself about the various sources of government money that are almost certainly available for capable entrepreneurs pursuing space-based ambitions.

One of my first contributions to the Space Economy was a paper entitled "Rethinking public-private space travel." My choice of subject wasn't accidental. From my initial exposure to the Space Economy at Astrobotic, I saw just how important government cooperation was—and would continue to be—in commercial space efforts. Just as the World Wide Web emerged directly from the military-funded ARPANET, the Space Economy's roots in government run deep and probably always will.

Defense contractors are still dependent on the government to operate. When I wrote my paper over a decade ago, SpaceX was in the same boat, though that has changed to an extent. Even today, however, most new companies that launch in the Space Economy do so with some form of government involvement and support. The very first dollars they use to conduct early research and build their first prototypes come not from private investors but from public agencies. In the United States, this means NASA, the U.S. Space Force, or one of the many other parts of the American government actively funding space-related research or serving as first customers to promising space startups.

This isn't going to change anytime soon. For more than 60 years, space was the exclusive domain of world powers. Even now, most major players in the Space Economy work closely with or rely on government agencies in one form or another. Moreover, outer space remains highly disputed territory. There is no global consensus over who should be allowed to operate in space or what they should be allowed to do once they're up there. Considering the dangers involved not just in launch and landing but also the military implications—more on those in Chapter 10— the Space Economy is an area of entrepreneurship in which the consequences of "move fast and break things" can be measured in megatons.

As an entrepreneur, chances are you'll be interacting with one government and possibly several. As we'll see in Chapter 6, it took the work of many political leaders and government administrators over the years to remove the roadblocks that prevented the Space Economy from flourishing in the United States. Forward-thinking efforts to encourage entrepreneurship by a government bureaucracy will always be a rare phenomenon, so keep the government factor front of mind. Administrations change, and so do the policies, programs, and regulations they champion. Just as a marketplace evolves over time, so does the political climate.

Defense contractors once held a death grip over government contracts. These legacy organizations acted as antibodies against innovation, fending off commercial space applications that threatened the steady flow of government pork. For decades, the contractors were successful in doing this. In part, Elon Musk succeeded in breaking their stranglehold because he played by the no-holds-barred rules of Silicon Valley. On the day of a crucial vote, for example, Musk put a Falcon 1 rocket on a flatbed truck and parked it in front of the House of Representatives. Publicly advocating on your company's behalf this way is part and parcel of the entrepreneurial process. Today, SpaceX maintains a massive lobbying arm. When NASA doled out a pork-barrel contract to a SpaceX competitor with an inferior offering, SpaceX leaped into the fray, suing NASA—its own, best customer—and winning.

Once you get a startup off the ground, you can look into joining the Commercial Spaceflight Federation, a lobbying group that represents hundreds of commercial space companies. The Federation gathers resources from member companies and uses that money to pursue the legislative priorities voted on by its constituents.

We'll explore the public-private aspect of the Space Economy more fully in Chapter 6. For now, it's enough to know that going after government funding—and learning more about the political landscape along the way—is one of the first steps any aspiring entrepreneur in the Space Economy needs to take.

Raising Capital

Well-understood businesses generally deliver expected returns. An experienced investor can look at foot traffic and demographics and determine the potential profit of a franchise restaurant down to the nickel. A relatively safe investment, but a limited one.

Investing at the edge of technological innovation carries a larger risk than opening a taco shop but promises a much larger potential upside. New tech is unknown and, therefore, unlimited by the status quo.

Renting out shared office space is a well-understood business with slim profit margins and many obstacles to growth. Rebrand yourself as a tech company, as Adam Neumann did with WeWork, and you can attract billions from international investors like SoftBank. It's a neat trick, and one that can work in your favor as a founder in the Space Economy. There is robust investor interest in technology with space applications or services that rely on space tech to serve ground-based customers. Unlike many other areas today, the investment dollars are there. Never lose sight of the fact that no one, including experienced investors, can say with any certainty just how high this ride will go. To secure investors, lead with space.

With the right customers in mind and a crack founding team assembled, it may be time to raise capital—if, and only if, the window of opportunity is limited and you have to grow quickly. This is why Dan Ceperley and his colleagues spun LeoLabs out from SRI International as a startup: "We needed to make a substantial investment in new hardware," Ceperley said. "Building radars around the world costs money. Because of the excitement investors now had about space, we could actually raise that capital. To do it effectively, however, we needed a new entity for investors to put their money into."

For many Space Economy startups, venture capital (VC) is the sensible approach. Planet Labs chose VC in particular for a reason: "We looked at RapidEye," Robbie Schingler told me. "German entrepreneurs conceived of the idea of a subscription-based monitoring service for agriculture back in 1999, but only launched in 2009 by relying on structured finance from banks. Thanks to the financial crisis, the banks insisted on repayment and RapidEye went bankrupt. One of their resellers bought them, and then we bought the reseller. Now we're doing what RapidEye wanted to do."

Securing sufficient runway is crucial: "If you're a first mover in a new frontier," Schingler said. "It's good not to over-stretch yourself so that one failure means you're dead. We always raised money when we didn't need it in order to have longevity. It's hard to build something."

Before you pitch investors, do the math: Is this idea physically feasible? Find someone with the necessary skill set to confirm this for you if you lack the requisite technical skills yourself. Regardless of your enthusiasm, don't wave away concerns about mass, thrust, and momentum. Far too many entrepreneurs pitch VC firms like ours without doing basic, back-of-the-envelope calculations to verify their ideas. We shouldn't be able to kill your concept with a calculator. If your business won't work because of something as well-established as, let's say, Newton's second law of motion, figure that out on your own time, not in a pitch meeting. You won't get a second one. The better you become at ruling out the impossible, the more likely you are to raise funding for the probable.

Preparation is key, but forget the formal business plan. It's a relic. If you want to wow investors, start working on the problem instead. Before seeking a single dollar of investment, have those early conversations with potential customers we discussed earlier. All you need for those is enough of a prototype to have a meaningful discussion. Whether you're sitting down with a telecom, a government agency, or a mobile phone marketing firm, there has to be enough meat on the bone for the customer to see what you have in mind, judge its potential, identify any flaws, and decide whether they'd pay.

The right prototype depends on the nature of your idea and the technical skill set your team brings to the table. It might be a primitive but functional device, a 3D-printed mock-up, or a diagram clearly laying out your business model. Famously, Southwest Airlines began as a sketch on a bar napkin. Its founders weren't designing a new kind of airplane. They were proposing a new business model for planes already in service. The napkin was enough to get to the next step.

In short, you don't need a fully operational satellite in orbit to talk to potential customers. To pitch software, use wireframes to illustrate the user interface and some of the potential output. If the hardware components you plan to use are commercially available, a mock-up will suffice. If you plan to develop novel components from scratch, detailed plans or schematics that stand up to professional scrutiny are a good first step.

As a venture capitalist, I find it useful to talk to a startup's potential customers and ask them whether they're interested in buying the product and, if so, why. Once it became clear that customers were interested in Violet Labs, investors became interested, too. Hoag and Curtis took a considered approach to the seed round, led by Space Capital: "We wanted diversity," Hoag explained. "We didn't want to be just a space-focused company. In order for our product to be really delightful for engineers to use, it should be appealing and valuable to a variety of engineers across industries, not just in aerospace. It was important to reflect that diversity in our selection of investors, as well as in the diversity of underrepresented groups in tech. That's deeply important to us and will be a strong theme in our company moving forward."

Choosing the right investors for your business is almost as important as choosing the right customers and co-founders: "I had a call with another founder about one of our investors," Anna Volkova of Regrow told me. "He said, 'How did you get them to invest?' He was asking the wrong question. The real question, I told him, was, '*Why* do you want them to invest? How are they going to add value?' As a founder, it's you and your investors in the boardroom making decisions about where the company is going. Do they grasp the concept of what you're trying to build? Can they offer expertise on when you need to make a specific hire? When to go to market? When to grow your engineering team? That's what matters. Founders go through much of their decision-making together with their consortium of investors. You want the right people in the room. It's literally that phrase: vested interest. You want the best people to have a vested interest in your success."

Remember, however, that you should only raise funding if your idea is vulnerable. If you have time to bootstrap it yourself, do that instead. Many software solutions that rely on the cloud and don't need much in the way of staff or infrastructure can grow quickly without outside funding of any kind. If you can realize your idea in this way, or at least get to the next stage of development without a major outlay of funds, consider pursuing the business as a side project until you build momentum. This reduces your personal financial risk, which gives you more runway to pivot until you find product-market fit. If you need capital down the road, investors will be more interested if you already have a customer base and steady revenue. At that point, they can help you get to the next stage.

If, however, you must seize a market opportunity before vultures swoop in and carve it out from under you, raise capital and use that money to scale up as quickly as possible. A startup is a company designed to grow fast. To achieve that rapid growth, you must make something many people want and then reach out and serve those people. If you get growth, everything else falls into place. In fact, growth is a useful compass for nearly every decision you face as an entrepreneur.

Venture capital is a tool to help startups grow faster. Each successive financing round is a critical evaluation point at which your company will live or die. With sufficient planning and preparation, you can significantly increase your chances of passing through each round successfully.

That said, you can do everything right and still fail.

Failing Forward

Most startups fail. According to some accounts, startup success rates hover between 10 and 20 percent over the long term. Believe it or not, this is a good thing. A startup is a kind of laboratory for determining whether a certain idea or set of ideas is viable. The beauty of a complete failure is that it delivers a conclusive test result. Assuming you run a tight ship, keep burn to a minimum, and stick to realistic goals, a failure in the marketplace proves that the idea you have lacks merit. Time to move on. Failure means you can set your idea down with a clear heart and move on to something with more potential.

As a VC, I like to see this kind of failure on a founder's resume. In fact, I encourage a fail-forward mentality among founders. The real risk for a founding team is a good-enough idea, something that generates enough profit to be self-sustaining but not much more than that. Entrepreneurship is an engine of economic progress. In return for shouldering a greater amount of risk, founders and investors get a shot at creating something of enormous value to the world: hockey-stick growth—a paradigm shift. If that envisioned Ferrari putters along like a golf cart, it poses a quandary. Accept a mediocre but profitable operation for what it is? Or cut bait and cast around for a bigger fish?

Smart VCs are more likely to back an entrepreneur with a well-executed whiff on a resume than one who has never taken a swing. We like action-oriented entrepreneurs who have tried things and learned from their mistakes along the way. A founder with a success but no failures may have gotten lucky the first time. Worse, they may be convinced that the next time will be just as easy. We're much more interested in a battle-hardened entrepreneur with an intimate understanding of the challenge—and a chip on their shoulder to do better next time.

***

Hopefully, this overview has given you a better understanding of the road from a promising idea to a living, breathing business in the Space Economy. There's a difference between telling and showing, however. The best practices laid out in this chapter are one thing—the lived reality of entrepreneurship is another.

"What I wish someone had told me is that you really have to pick and choose which advice you listen to," Lucy Hoag of Violet Labs told me. "My advice would be to have more confidence in your own thoughts and your own path forward. Plenty of advice out there is useful, but you have to do your own thing and trust yourself."

We've seen the importance of studying the political and regulatory landscape as it applies to space. Out of historical context, the picture is complicated and often baffling. However, if you learn how we got here from the days of the Apollo missions as seen through the eyes of the people in the industry at the time, you will have a much better understanding of today's Space Economy—and how it will evolve moving forward. Read on.

CHAPTER 6

From Apollo to SpaceX and Beyond: The Fall and Rise of American Space Ambitions and the Future of Public– Private Partnerships

At the beginning of this book, I said I would explain the central mystery of the decline—and subsequent public– private rebirth—of U.S. space efforts and, in tandem, the Space Economy as a global phenomenon.

So, what happened? How is it possible that, in the same decades that America rebounded from crime waves and economic malaise to achieve new heights of economic success, NASA went from the extraordinary Apollo Moon missions to the overpriced, underperforming, and spectacularly unsafe Space Shuttle program, which led to not one but two fatal disasters, and, by the time it was retired in 2011, had become synonymous in the minds of many with government inefficiency and waste?

Even as America's space capabilities declined after Apollo, the seeds of today's Space Economy were being planted during each subsequent government administration and across a shifting geopolitical landscape. Without the efforts of several far-sighted entrepreneurs, investors, and yes, even government leaders, we would never have seen the recent wave of entrepreneurship and innovation that has restored America's space ambitions and enhanced its capabilities. The most visible part of this resurgence—SpaceX—is just the tip of an iceberg of dedicated effort by many individuals over several decades. They deserve more credit for their contributions, as we'll see.

Once this story has been told, I will also explore the uneasy, constantly evolving, but ultimately fruitful relationship between companies in the Space Economy and governments worldwide. In a hopeful shift, most are steering their efforts away from direct space exploration and toward the regulation of space to create a peaceful and equitable environment for private enterprise to pursue its own ends.

Rising from the Ashes of Apollo

On April 12, 1981, astronauts John Young and Robert Crippen flew Space Shuttle *Columbia* into orbit. STS-1 was the first Space Shuttle launch, and five-year-old Peter Marquez was watching at home.

"Seeing the very first Space Shuttle launch left an indelible mark on my brain," Marquez told me. "That was pretty much it from there. Anything having to do with space, I was all about it." Naturally, Marquez went to space camp as a teenager. Later on, he earned a master's degree from the Space Policy Institute at the George Washington University.

Marquez's first stop after graduate school was the Pentagon. After seven years working on classified space programs with entities like the Air Force and the Department of Defense, Marquez spent three years as the director of Space Policy for the National Security Council, advising both the Bush and Obama administrations on space policy. Work in the commercial Space Economy followed, as we'll see in a later chapter.

Over the course of his career, Marquez has been a powerhouse in space policy, both in the United States and worldwide. Even after entering the private sector, Marquez has been asked to continue advising on government policy. He has contributed to the 2015 Space Resource Exploration and Utilization Act and the 2020 U.S. National Space Policy. Looking back, Marquez has his own opinion about what brought Apollo down to Earth.

"Understanding the American space program is easy once you unlock the secret code," Marquez said. "Political will. Realpolitik. Once you add that in, you can understand every space decision at a macro level. From 1961 through 1973—the Mercury, Gemini, and Apollo missions—that was realpolitik. The Cold War. Using space as a tool of political power to show which system was the better system. That's all that was."

"Once we landed on the Moon," Marquez said, "and the Russians essentially admitted defeat in the Space Race, space could no longer be used for that strategy. NASA was adrift, trying to figure out what to do next. There was no specific target." The impossible dream had been achieved—how could they top it?

Things grew bleak. Thanks to a series of failures and accidents, several planned Apollo missions were canceled in the 1960s and 1970s. Then NASA shuttered the whole program, spurring a downturn across the aerospace and defense industries.

"There were still missions and needs for science and national security," Marquez said. "So you get the Shuttle program, a very expensive compromise between NASA and the Air Force. Since the Shuttle didn't fully meet Air Force requirements, they ended up divesting themselves of the project completely, leaving NASA manacled with an incredibly expensive project in need of justification."

Despite the Shuttle's many limitations, the Nixon administration made the decision to rely on it entirely for America's future launch capability. Not only did this curtail the kinds of missions that could be undertaken—a return to the Moon was off the table, for one—it also left ELV (Expendable Launch Vehicle) manufacturers without a path forward.

In 1984, a glimmer of hope appeared on the horizon. President Ronald Reagan's State of the Union address in January struck a bold chord by identifying space as America's "next frontier":

> The Space Age is barely a quarter of a century old, but already we've pushed civilization forward with our advances in science and technology. Opportunities and jobs will multiply as we cross new thresholds of knowledge and reach deeper into the unknown. Our progress in space—taking giant steps for all mankind—is a tribute to American teamwork and excellence. Our finest minds in government, industry, and academia have all pulled together. And we can be proud to say: We are first; we are the best; and we are so because we're free.

That bit about freedom at the end was a not-so-subtle jab at the Soviet Union. Though it had ultimately been defeated in the Space Race, Russia remained a major threat to the United States, both militarily and geopolitically.

In his address, Reagan announced the decision to build the International Space Station to "permit quantum leaps in our research in science, communications, in metals, and in lifesaving medicines which could be manufactured only in space." Then, the former movie star waxed romantic:

> Just as the oceans opened up a new world for clipper ships and Yankee traders, space holds enormous potential for commerce today. The market for space transportation could surpass our capacity to develop it. Companies interested in putting payloads into space must have ready access to private-sector launch services. The Department of Transportation will help an expendable launch services industry to get off the ground. We'll soon implement a number of executive initiatives, develop proposals to ease regulatory constraints, and, with NASA's help, promote private-sector investment in space.

If this speech had been delivered 20 years later, it would seem prescient in retrospect. As it happened, however, little of this came to pass, for reasons that will soon become clear. However, the 1984 State of the Union is as good a place as any to mark the birth of today's commercial space industry. Reagan planted an important seed, even if that seed would take far longer than it should have to germinate: "It takes a long time for these things to mature," Mike Griffin told me. Griffin was at the Applied Physics Laboratory at Johns Hopkins at the time of Reagan's speech and went on to become Administrator of NASA among other major roles. "It took a lot to get it done," Griffin said, "but that's where it started."

That year, Reagan signed a key piece of legislation, the Commercial Space Launch Act of 1984:

> One of the important objectives of my administration has been, and will continue to be, the encouragement of the private sector in commercial space endeavors . . . Enactment of this legislation is a milestone in our efforts to address the need of private companies interested in launching payloads to have ready access to space . . . We expect that a healthy ELV industry, as a complement to the Government's space transportation system, will produce a stronger, more efficient launch capability for the United States that will contribute to continued American leadership in space.

The new law put into effect "a comprehensive licensing mechanism enabling launch operators to comply quickly and efficiently with existing Federal regulations [to] act as a signal to private launch operators that this administration stands behind their efforts to open up this new area of space exploration." The Act also established the Office of Commercial Space Transportation (OCST), under the Department of Transportation.

The Reagan administration also reversed Nixon's decision to rely on the Shuttle for launch: "This alone saved the expendable launch vehicle industry, which was nearly dead," Scott Pace, Associate Administrator of NASA under George W. Bush, told me. "The Delta and Atlas rockets got a reprieve."

Though Reagan did a great deal to maintain and expand American launch capability beyond the Shuttle, NASA felt strongly that there would only ever be a certain amount of demand for launch no matter how cheap it became. As for the ISS, achieving "quantum leaps" in technological innovation wasn't the real purpose of the program from the perspective of many in the industry, including Space Capital's Tom Ingersoll.

"The purpose of the ISS," Ingersoll told me, "was to justify the Space Shuttle program and give it something to do." By this point, the Shuttle had been operational for three years, and even boosters of the program were struggling to make a case for its incredibly costly existence.

For all its flaws, however, the Space Shuttle stood for the possibility of space access becoming in some way routine. "Once you had routine space access," Pace said, "other things could spin off from it. Some of the advanced thinkers at NASA saw activities like servicing geostationary satellites and platforms as a possible back door to the Moon. Once you have a commercial reason to send people to geostationary orbit, the extra delta-v from there to the Moon is relatively minor." Unfortunately, getting into orbit with the Space Shuttle was both difficult and expensive—anything but routine.

Reagan also established the Space Defense Initiative Organization (SDIO), colloquially (and derisively) referred to as "Star Wars." SDIO's stated purpose was to create a defensive shield around the United States and its allies to prevent Russia from landing any of its vast arsenal of ICBMs in the case of a nuclear conflict. Star Wars called for the deployment of massive systems on the outermost edge of space technology: particle beams, space-based lasers, kinetic energy weapons, space planes. From its wildly ambitious goals to the nickname drawn from a movie blockbuster, Star Wars sounded to the American public just like science fiction. In a very real sense, it was. The U.S. government threw billions of dollars at SDIO not to build a missile-proof shield but to encourage a belief in the possibility that it would. According to Ingersoll, who had a front-row seat to the saga, the true motive of Star Wars was to pressure the Soviet Union. For this purpose, the threat only needed to be credible enough to incentivize the shaky Eastern Bloc to invest more and more funds in defense spending: nuclear weapons, the Mir space station, and other big, expensive projects. Ideally, this would exacerbate its desperate fiscal straits and ultimately cause its collapse.

As intended, the illusion that the United States would be able to protect itself from nuclear weapons did indeed push the USSR to overspend on space programs even as its people starved. Looking back, an argument could be made that Star Wars contributed to the fall of the Iron Curtain as much as any other single factor.

While Star Wars may have established America's geopolitical dominance, the loss of a rival played havoc with the U.S. space program. Government spending on space had always been a tough sell to taxpayers. Competition with the Soviet Union had always been instrumental in justifying the investment. How would politicians make the case for NASA now? As soon as the Soviet Union collapsed, Star Wars essentially went away. Meanwhile, by succeeding so thoroughly, the Star Wars strategy had created a new problem: Russia had a surplus of engineers who all possessed exceedingly dangerous expertise in rocketry, satellites, and nuclear weapon design.

"We had a proliferation problem," Peter Marquez said. "Realpolitik raised its head again. We didn't want Russian scientists going all over the world. So we created a jobs program. Like the Tennessee Valley Authority during the Great Depression, we built the International Space Station. Get the Russians on board, keep them busy, and create a reason for the Shuttle to exist while you're at it." This also explains America's sudden involvement in the Mir space station and reliance on Soyuz launch vehicles.

"We were funding all of these Russian technologists when the country collapsed in order to keep them employed," Ingersoll said. This "white-collar welfare," as he put it, took the steam out of space commercialization. There was now a strong incentive beyond mere technological progress to rely on government-led efforts.

Reign of the Defense Contractors

"The way Shuttle pricing had worked, private carriers couldn't make money because they couldn't compete with the Shuttle," Scott Pace said. "Once the Shuttle was taken out of the market by policy as a result of *Challenger*, there was some breathing room. The expendable launch guys had a way forward again."

In 1991, SDIO asked McDonnell Douglas to develop a single-stage-to-orbit, reusable launch vehicle (SSTO RLV). Working at McDonnell Douglas under former Apollo astronaut Pete Conrad, Tom Ingersoll played a key role in developing what became the Delta Clipper Experimental (DC-X). A few years later at Lockheed Martin, the General Dynamics team that had developed the Atlas rocket went to work on Lockheed's own contender: the X-33 VentureStar.

General Dynamics's reusable Atlas program had run into trouble as it evolved from a government rocket to a commercial system. However, Navy admiral and Apollo astronaut T. K. Mattingly had come on board and gotten things under control. Under Mattingly's leadership, Atlas became the most reliable launch vehicle available—a relative statement but still a significant feat. After Martin Marietta bought General Dynamics and Lockheed bought Martin, the new Lockheed Martin put Mattingly in charge of VentureStar. Pete Conrad and Tom Ingersoll at McDonnell Douglas were further along with the DC-X. They even had a working prototype. However, they had a problem. McDonnell Douglas was approaching a merger with Boeing. In the interim, the company refused to commit more than a paltry $10 million to the DC-X program.

At the time, Lockheed Martin was selling Titan rockets to NASA and the Air Force for as much as a billion dollars each. These billion-dollar rockets were failing regularly with billion-dollar payloads aboard. If this seems crazy now, Ingersoll says it was business as usual at the time. The Air Force and NASA had their hands tied by their own contracting rules. Essentially, the government paid defense contractors for effort, not success. None of the defense contractors had a genuine incentive to make progress.

One consequence of this bureaucratic quagmire can be seen in the sad fate of VentureStar. As Ingersoll and Conrad tried to win NASA's support for the DC-X, Lockheed Martin CEO Norman Augustine called T. K. Mattingly daily asking what the company could do to beat McDonnell Douglas to the punch. As Mattingly later told Ingersoll, Augustine committed to investing a billion dollars in VentureStar. Compared with the paltry $10 million McDonnell Douglas had bet on the DC-X, Lockheed Martin's enormous commitment to VentureStar made it the obvious choice for NASA.

However, once NASA gave the SSTO RLV contract to Lockheed Martin, the promised billion never materialized. In fact, Mattingly discovered that Norman Augustine, his own boss, the guy who had called him every day to convey his enthusiasm for VentureStar, was no longer taking his phone calls.

"That was the state of the industry," Ingersoll told me. "The big aerospace companies did not want any kind of commercialization. They were fighting it tooth and nail. Maybe I'm jaded, but it sure seemed like Augustine only said he'd put a billion into VentureStar so he could kill it before it threatened his Titan IV revenue stream."

Though McDonnell Douglas was closer to a production-ready vehicle when it lost out to Lockheed Martin, the picture there wasn't fundamentally different. When Conrad and Ingersoll pushed for a lower-cost commercial approach to vehicle development, McDonnell Douglas aerospace leader Bill Olson made his priorities clear: "Why would I want to do low-cost space when I can sell all the expensive stuff we make?" This, in Ingersoll's opinion, was how the government gravy train worked. You sold expensive stuff and killed anything that threatened your business model.

After Olson laid his cards on the table, Conrad and Ingersoll quit to form their own commercial space venture, and the DC-X program was shuttered.

The First Commercial Space Efforts

In the mid-90s, there had been a plan to issue a billion-dollar request for proposals to refresh NASA's satellite ground station network. However, Joe Rothenberg, NASA's associate administrator for space flight, decided it made no sense to invest in building assets when NASA could pay for services instead.

In 1998, Rothenberg successfully pushed for the Commercial Space Operations Contract (CSOC), a billion-dollar investment in commercially built ground stations. CSOC promised to greatly reduce costs by creating a marketplace that new companies could enter and marked the beginning of NASA's reliance on commercial space operations. Tom Ingersoll ended up running one of the companies in this new marketplace: a provider of commercial tracking, telemetry, and control services for spacecraft called Universal Space Network (USN). USN started as a subsidiary of Universal Space Lines, the company Ingersoll had co-founded with Pete Conrad, T. K. Mattingly, and Bruce McCaw after leaving McDonnell Douglas. (Behind the scenes, McCaw, co-founder of McCaw Cellular, was enormously influential in supporting early space companies as an investor, co-founder, and board member, leveraging his leadership, business experience, and network to support these initiatives.)

"The economics of USN were compelling," Ingersoll said, "when you realized that people were spending $10 million on a ground station and needed multiple ground stations, all of which needed people operating them. If you could find a way to automate some of that and then timeshare those ground stations across many different satellites, you had a classic buy-it-once, sell-it-a-thousand-times business model. USN wasn't a massive financial success, but we were profitable, and we sold it at a profit in 2011. Importantly, we also demonstrated to the industry that you really could outsource commercial space services."

Despite its success, USN remained an outlier for some time. NASA was deeply skeptical of the commercial potential of space. Its attitude in those days evokes IBM president Thomas Watson's 1943 assertion that the potential market for electronic computers amounted to "maybe five." To be fair, however, NASA had reason to be wary. In the mid-90s, Teledesic had announced grandiose plans for a low-Earth orbit (LEO) commercial broadband satellite internet constellation. Backed by Microsoft co-founder Bill Gates among others, Teledesic's failure struck a major blow to the idea of commercialization.

Why did most early commercialization efforts fail? One factor was a lack of intellectual diversity and commercial background. For example, when the DC-X program ended, its chief engineer, Jim French, went to Kistler Aerospace to work on a new launch vehicle. Though Kistler hired French along with other talented alums of the Apollo missions, Kistler itself was run by former government bureaucrats with little understanding of the requirements of private enterprise. According to Ingersoll, they simply didn't have the in-house expertise and business focus to complete a big engineering project on a budget. Beal Aerospace, another early private space company, had the business sense, but its engineering team misjudged the technical challenge of launch, pursuing a peroxide rocket solution that wasn't technologically feasible.

To succeed, a leader would clearly need to understand both the commercial and the engineering challenges. Ironically, the one entrepreneur who did came from another industry altogether: the internet.

For a period of time, Mike Griffin engaged in consulting work. One of his clients at the time was Elon Musk, who had just sold PayPal. Musk came to Griffin because he wanted to send a payload to Mars. "Musk's idea was to send a flower in a bell jar," Griffin told me, "and take a picture of it to show something growing on Mars." At the time, the most viable option for getting to the Red Planet was a Russian SS-18 "Satan" ICBM. Griffin accompanied Musk to Moscow, where the Russians, sensing a PayPal payday, demanded an outrageous fee. "They were trying to hold Elon hostage," Griffin said. "Elon told them he could do better. On the flight back, he decided to form SpaceX."

Prior to Musk's decision, Rocket Development Corporation (RDC), another subsidiary of Universal Space Lines, had made solid progress in developing a next-generation launch vehicle. However, the dot-com bubble had burst before it could raise a Series B round. If you were an ambitious entrepreneur looking to get your own rocket company at the time, the failing company presented a tempting target.

"Two groups took a serious look at RDC," Ingersoll said. "One led by Elon Musk and a second by Jeff Bezos." Just as the United States and Russia secured their own caches of German rocket scientists after World War II in Operation Paperclip, RDC's scientists and engineers were split between the two ambitious, deep-pocketed entrepreneurs. Each commanded enormous resources. Each intended to offer commercial launch services. But there was a crucial difference.

"Musk had the technical chops to understand how hard launch is," Ingersoll said, "and the vision to go one step at a time." Bezos had money and business acumen, but he was also busy running one of the largest and fastest-growing businesses in the world, forcing him to rely on the talent he'd hired out of Beal and Kistler: "Bezos lost time and money initially pursuing peroxide rockets," Ingersoll said. "The chemistry simply doesn't work."

Ingersoll sees both Musk and Bezos as catalysts of the Space Economy, just as Musk kick-started the electric car: "We had a ton of people building silly electric cars until one guy did it right, and that's what happened with launch services. Musk's success finally enabled competent teams to step forward and do things that people had said they couldn't do. We started moving forward."

Simultaneously, leaders at NASA were becoming converts not only to commercialization but also to a more ambitious view of space. The Space Shuttle *Columbia* accident played a role in changing perspectives.

"When the *Columbia* accident happened in the middle of assembling the International Space Station [ISS]," Scott Pace said, "it forced the question: 'Why are we risking humans going up and down and cycling around the Earth at all?' If we're going to do this, we need to play for higher stakes. The game needs to be worth the candle.' This led to a new vision for space exploration."

"When Mike Griffin was explaining the return to flight after the accident to President Bush," Pace said, "Griffin made it clear that even though NASA had done everything it could, things could still go wrong. There was a non-zero chance of another accident before we completed the ISS. The faces in the room went ashen: 'Are you kidding me?'"

"We asked the international partners whether they wanted to pause the station's assembly," Pace said. "We were at a stable point. We could stop without adding the international modules. But Chancellor Angela Merkel's position was, essentially, 'You have to try. We can't conduct other co-operations in the future if we give up now.' I credit Merkel for being the final drop on that scale. So President Bush said, 'These guys [the astronauts] are professionals. They understand the risks. We're completing the ISS for the honor of the United States.' Nobody else could make that decision. Bush made that decision." That just left the problem of getting an enormous amount of work done with a Shuttle program that was almost out of runway.

"When I walked into NASA," Mike Griffin said, "the Shuttle was going to be retired in 2010. We had a commitment from Congress, backed by the President, with fourteen other countries that we were going to finish the ISS. This meant I had to get the Shuttle back to flight. So, I put together a team and we crafted a plan for finishing the Space Station within the timeline that we were still allowed to fly the Shuttle. This meant eliminating all the utilization flights and focusing only on assembly flights. We figured that if we could get it done, we'd be able to utilize it later."

"Following the Columbia Accident Investigation Board," Griffin said, "we also had a non-negotiable requirement to separate crew from cargo. Future crew modules could have trunks like a car, but they couldn't be semi-trucks like the Space Shuttle. We had to figure out how to get cargo to the ISS with unmanned vehicles."

"At that time, Boeing and Lockheed were offering rocket launches at $300 million apiece," Griffin said. "The United States had commitments to deliver certain amounts of cargo per year to the Space Station, as did the Russians. I had to find new providers because we couldn't afford that price for delivering cargo."

New launch providers would also add much-needed resiliency: "*Columbia* pounded the value of dissimilar redundancy into people's minds," Scott Pace said. "The Russians bailed us out on the ISS after the accident. We had no way of supporting it without the Russians. That got the lesson into our bones."

"It was my judgment that the rocket industry could build a cargo rocket without the close supervision of the government," Griffin said. "I am a free market capitalist and I believe in competition. Yes, capitalism needs to be governed so that people don't become criminals, but the free market works well when there is a balance between customers and suppliers. When there are no commercial customers, the market doesn't work at all."

"There are no commercial customers for 9G fighter airplanes, for example," Griffin said. "If the country wants them, they must be provided by industry under contract, with no market discipline to control them. Once you've signed up to buy an F-35, you're a hostage to Lockheed. So those products have to be closely supervised by expert government people. That requirement was often lacking, as we've seen with the F-35. At the other end of the spectrum is the iPhone. I don't want to deal with a government-developed iPhone. The government can buy iPhones from industry."

"Then there are things in the middle," Griffin continued. "By 2005, it was my judgment that rockets were somewhere in the middle. There was a robust commercial market for rockets in the form of communication satellites and imagery satellites. But commercial satellites couldn't exist without a government-supported defense industrial base. The market for commercial communications was there, but you wouldn't be able to develop a business case around that without the defense base. Commercial satellites by themselves wouldn't work. They represent a marginal use of an activity that is part of the national security establishment of the United States."

"Intelligent government policy can make good use of that industrial base to develop commercial activities," Griffin said. "Think of what the U.S. economy would look like without the development of transcontinental railroads, the interstate highway system, and, in the modern era, Federal air traffic control. Can you imagine a state-by-state or even company-by-company air traffic control system? I'm a commercial pilot, and I fly in the air traffic control system almost every week. I cannot imagine how that could work. That said, the ends don't justify the means. The construction of the transcontinental railroad involved landmark corruption lawsuits that went on for decades and resulted in personal hardships being visited on people in ways that should never have been allowed."

"As time and technology evolve," Griffin said, "there's a moving boundary between what requires government support and what can be done by private industry. When computers first got started, that was a government proposition. Now I don't want the government anywhere near them. When rockets first got started, it was a government proposition. In 2005, the government still needed to be a part of that industry, but there was a piece that private industry could develop and possibly even close a business case."

"Once we set up COTS [NASA's Commercial Orbital Transportation Services program]," Griffin said. "I persuaded the Office of Management and Budget to allow me to put $500 million into it, $250 million each for two providers. Ballparking it, I thought $250 million was about a third of what a private company would need to develop a cargo-class launch vehicle to resupply the Station. If the government anted up a third, that would allow them to attract private capital and develop the rocket commercially without the government prescribing the design. The idea was mine, but Scott Pace took care of the policy aspects and orchestrated the budget. I just had the idea and championed it as its public face. As NASA Administrator, my main task was to get the Shuttle returned to flight and craft an architecture to get us back to the Moon."

"We ran a competition," Griffin said. "The companies had to bring a business plan that included a rocket design. However, we weren't going to scrub their rocket designs except at a very high level. The whole idea was to *not* prescribe the design. Let the supplier do that. When the government buys a fleet of cars for a military base, they run a competition between GM, Ford, and Chrysler, and take the best deal. That's what I was trying to do. And, based on the submissions, we picked two winners: SpaceX and Kistler."

"SpaceX and Kistler were the two best proposals," Scott Pace, who advised on the decision, said. "Their proposals offered the best value for the money while being technically credible. Orbital [Orbital Sciences Corporation, now part of Northrop Grumman] was number three by a small margin. There was a gap. When Kistler missed milestones, however, we didn't feel bad about turning to Orbital and moving forward."

"In the end, SpaceX and Orbital both got to the finish line with Cargo Dragon and Cygnus," Griffin said, "and both vehicles are still flying."

"Look," Griffin said, "as NASA Administrator, I couldn't make policy. I could only execute it. If I wasn't going to have a Shuttle and I wasn't going to have a manned space vehicle that could deliver cargo and I couldn't afford what Lockheed and Boeing wanted to charge for their rockets, what *was* I going to do? I had this idea, and it worked out."

"There were limitations, of course," Griffin continued. "Center of gravity limitations, so you couldn't load up as much as you wanted. In contrast to SpaceX, Orbital had a supply chain with stuff coming from around the world, including Ukraine, which made them vulnerable in other ways. It was imperfect. But did we get value for our money? Yes, we did. Not as much as we'd hoped, but we got other people to focus on the problem."

This experience taught NASA the value of hedging its bets. When the next administration leveraged the same COTS contracting mechanism for a crewed mission, they again selected two providers: SpaceX and Boeing. Lori Garver, Deputy Administrator of NASA under President Obama, felt good about Musk's chances, but she knew better than to bet everything on one horse: "As SpaceX came along, we saw somebody who might really be able to pull it off," Garver told me in 2019. "However, this wasn't the first time we'd thought that. Kistler, Beal—we'd supported them all. When we bet on SpaceX, it was a risk, but everyone in the administration believed in letting privately-led innovation advance the space program."

The Evolution of American Space Policy

"When I was crafting the National Space Policy," Peter Marquez told me, "I incorporated language to support regulation that would allow the commercial space industry to grow." However, not everyone in the administration agreed with this approach: "It was like, 'How could you put this stuff in here? Why are you supporting the commercial industry so much? There isn't one.'"

Many powerful figures within the Department of Defense believed that relying on private companies to deliver critical government payloads to orbit threatened national security. "We don't want to put our stuff on those rockets," they told the White House, according to Marquez. "They're going to blow up. We don't trust them. You're detracting from our real missions."

SpaceX soon vindicated Marquez's belief in the potential for a commercial space industry: "Now you look at the National Space Policy and go, 'Yeah, of course. You'd be stupid not to include that stuff.' But at the time, we were seen as heretics. There was no talk of satellite constellations. If you suggested launching a hundred satellites, people would say 'ridiculous.' Today, people are like, 'Oh, a five-thousand-satellite constellation? Yawn.' It's astounding what's happened over the last fifteen years."

The policy changes that propelled the rise of the Space Economy only happened because of a new mindset. The traditionalists in the Department of Defense believed that "government people should be supporting government programs," according to Marquez. He and his allies, including Scott Pace and Mike Griffin at NASA and Damon Wells in the White House Office of Science and Technology Policy, saw things differently. "We believed that the focus on government was the true national security threat," he said. "We weren't building new capability. We weren't building a broader economy. We weren't building new IP. We weren't building new technologies. We weren't exporting things. If you look at what the U.S. launch industry was like in 2007, it's clear we were giving up our place in the space community by foregoing commercial launch."

"On our side, we believed that commercial launch capability would be our salvation," Marquez said, "both in terms of national security and of economic development." Relying on private enterprise for technological progress is an unabashedly American tactic and Marquez knew he wasn't the first to see that: "When I was writing the National Space Policy," Marquez said, "I kept a copy of Reagan's first space policy on my desk. It emphasized what commercial industry could do. Since then, we had gone away from all these things that were supposedly hard and fast rules of the American ethos: trust industry, trust capitalism, trust technology. In 2010, I didn't think I was doing anything revolutionary. I was just going back in time to the 1980s."

Today, international cooperation is the name of the game: "Back in the days of the Apollo program," Scott Pace said, "it was like, 'Look, how cool I am, I can do something nobody else can.' Today, it's, 'Look how cool I am, everybody wants to be in my club.'"

"The United States has a security dilemma," Pace said. "We're dependent upon space, both militarily and economically, as much as, if not more than, Great Britain was dependent on the ocean in the seventeenth through nineteenth centuries. We're dependent on space, but we don't own it. We have no sovereign rights to it. We can't control it or put a fence around it. So if we're going to secure our interests, we need to persuade other sovereign states that it's in their best interests to align with us of their own free will. To do that, they need to be part of an enterprise that they can meaningfully participate in."

"I love Mars," Pace said, "but a Mars program doesn't provide us with different price points for countries to come in at. With the Moon, I can have countries with varying levels of space capability participate meaningfully. I can have a multibillion-dollar Lunar rover from Japan. I can get a Mexican rover on an Astrobotic Lunar Lander, which makes Mexico the first Latin American country on the Moon. That kind of thing gives us engagement. It allows us to shape the international environment. I'm not a commercial space idealogue. A Lunar program advances our national security and economic interests through commercial and international partnerships."

"We don't know if all this is going to work," Pace said. "If anybody says they know, they're wrong. You don't know until you do it. We don't know where humans can go, what they can do, what they can survive, or what makes sense economically. This is exploration. We don't know, but we're going to find out. The important thing is, if there is going to be a human future in space, I want the United States and its allies and friends there. I want it to have the values of the Enlightenment: the rule of law, democracy, human rights."

"There will be others in space who don't share those values," Pace said. "That's fine. They have a right to be in space as sovereign countries and human beings. But I don't want to leave space to them. I don't want them shaping the rules of that environment on their own. I want to shape that environment with my friends to preserve the values we hold dear. The same idea applies to the seas, the air, cyberspace, international trade, you name it. The rules get made by the people who show up, not the ones who stay behind."

Space Force

"As early as the 1950s," Peter Marquez said, "there was an argument about who would be in charge of space: the Department of Defense, the Navy, the Air Force, or the Army. There was even discussion of a 'Space Force,' but people laughed about the idea. 'Come on, there isn't any capability yet.' So the idea of a Space Force isn't new, but it only got traction about a decade ago."

Although the 2019 establishment of the U.S. Space Force generated plenty of skepticism, even mirth—Marquez himself was a consultant on the Netflix comedy *Space Force* starring Steve Carell—he believes it was a smart move. "Now you've got a focused chief of space operations whose sole job is to make sure that our national security space systems work," Marquez said. "All the work that General John Raymond has done to create a coalition for space security has been extremely helpful. You wouldn't have gotten this kind of progress if space were still an Air Force activity."

"There will always be threats to the U.S. and its allies in space," Marquez said. "In fact, I think we're on better footing today than in the days of the Cold War despite the proliferation of threats across the spectrum. We've got more allies and supporters on board with the idea of safe space operations. Questions like, what is space sustainability? What do good people do in space? What is considered bad behavior? What are resilient capabilities that we can build together? I'm not saying everything's perfect, but I'm actually very positive about our ability to respond to new threats."

"The Space Force was not something that was pulled out of the air at the last minute," Pace said. "It had been cooking for three decades. Since the 2007 Chinese antisatellite test, we had been seeing more and more threats. To its credit, the Obama administration had put serious money into resilience. They had put a down payment toward it. Then we came in and said, 'This is bad. We're looking at a crisis. Space is central, and we need to focus on it. Congress is pressing here. We need a Space Force.' We laid out the options, the President picked one, and away we went."

When Public and Private Collide

Catalyzed by SpaceX and no longer completely dependent on government support, private industry is doing what it does best: drive progress. Governments, meanwhile, are doing what they always do when commerce drives progress: struggle to keep up.

"We need to address whether our current international forums for dispute resolution and regulatory enforcement can keep pace with commercial activity," Peter Marquez said. "It's going to be a real problem if we have to rely on these international and domestic regulatory bodies to make decisions. Industry moves at a much faster pace than governments do. If companies have to wait on governments and international bodies to make regulations or handle enforcement, we're going to create a lot more problems than opportunities in the near future."

"For one major example," Marquez continued, "Article VI of the Outer Space Treaty says that a nation has to authorize and supervise what their companies and citizens do in space. Right now, America has an established process for remote sensing and one for communications. Once you get outside those bounds, we provide no regulatory guidance whatsoever. Investors don't like legal and regulatory uncertainty. No one wants to think that a new law could wipe out their entire investment."

As with all entrepreneurial activity, regulatory uncertainty doesn't impede progress as much as drive it elsewhere. Companies pursuing space activity that isn't covered by existing regulations repatriate: "Luxembourg has picked up the mantle," Marquez said. "'You want a flexible, responsive regulatory environment? Luxembourg will take care of you.' We're at risk of wasting all the work we've put into creating a commercial space capability by forcing it overseas because we can't get our regulations to match our investments. That's a real concern."

"Internationally," Marquez continued, "companies that are pouring billions of dollars into satellite communication systems rely on the UN's International Telecommunication Union, which takes years to make decisions. It's completely out of sync with the commercial market. Will we see the reemergence of a Venetian trading model, where private companies negotiate with international bodies directly at the level of nation-states? These are questions we haven't begun to explore."

"The U.S. has a real opportunity here to work with its allies and partners," Marquez said. "Just as NASA created the Artemis Accords to establish responsible behavior on the Moon, the Department of Commerce could lay the groundwork for how commercial systems will operate in space. That way, we can avoid old maritime problems like flags of convenience. There's a reason cruise ships are flagged in certain countries—the regulatory restrictions in those countries are less strict. If we had Artemis Accords for commercial space, we could get ahead of these issues." Marquez isn't particularly optimistic about this possibility, however: "At a certain point, we need to stop looking to governments to be leaders and see which companies will take the initiative. Companies now have capabilities on par with nations, and some companies have capabilities far exceeding that of many nations."

In the United States, the lack of regulatory focus makes commerce more difficult. Dan Ceperley of LeoLabs, for one, thinks the government can play a more helpful role than it currently does.

"There is a need for a civil space agency to govern space," Ceperley said. "The Space Force likes to point out that it's not a regulator and cannot govern space. That's a strong argument for the Commerce Department playing a leading role in that area." This kind of intervention would be far from unprecedented. "In many other sectors, like transportation, communications, or financial services," Ceperley continued, "the government shifted out of a role of providing infrastructure and into a role of setting policy, guidelines, regulations, and enforcement. This keeps things vibrant by ensuring a level playing field for an industry. That approach would go a long way towards promoting the U.S. space sector and making it very healthy."

Given the rapid pace of innovation, governments have a responsibility to adapt regulatory structures to keep pace with that development. To be effective, regulations must ensure safe and sustainable operations in space without stifling innovation or impeding the growth of promising new applications with tangible benefits.

If you are doing anything truly innovative at your company, engage with regulators early so that the regulatory process is already well underway when you're ready to launch your product or service. "At Kymeta," Nathan Kundtz, CEO of Rendered. ai, said, "we faced challenges around FCC regulations in which some of the FCC rules for antennas didn't take into account the latest technological innovations we'd made. We did an engineering analysis of the antennas we wanted to use and worked closely with the regulators at the FCC. Supported by that analysis, we proposed new rules and the FCC modified their regulations."

"If the rules haven't caught up yet, it does take work to change them, but it's not insurmountable," Kundtz continued. "Entrepreneurs say, 'Oh well, those are the regulations.' But if you talk to regulators, you'll find that they're interested in learning more. They want to know about the latest technology. It's their job to make sure that the regulations support what's happening in the ecosystem."

This doesn't mean the FCC is always so accommodating: "The reality is, they have to think about everything in the ecosystem, not just the newest thing. Sometimes, there's a conflict. But they do love hearing about what you're doing and they will respond. They move at the pace of government, but working with the FCC is still much faster than getting new legislation passed."

***

As Peter Marquez pointed out, investors don't like uncertainty. As you can see repeatedly throughout this narrative, commercial space efforts took a step forward every time government gave more reign to market forces.

Today, the Space Economy is attracting an enormous amount of capital, from venture capital firms like Space Capital on one end of the spectrum all the way to the big banks and retail investors on the other. Our investment thesis has always been that success requires intimate knowledge of the terrain.

In the next chapter, we will look more closely at the unique challenges of investing in the Space Economy.

CHAPTER 7

Buy Low, Sell Very High: Investing in the Space Economy

Whether you work in satellite manufacturing or software development, rocket design or real estate, what's happening in space will become increasingly relevant to your work and industry over the next decade. The Space Economy is on track to becoming the dominant source of growth across the global economy.

No one can ignore or downplay this phenomenon. Financial analysts, venture capitalists, and investment bankers aren't the only ones who must understand how these markets work and where these industries might be going. Space professionals should also understand the investment side if they hope to navigate the choppy waters ahead. And, since space technologies are the next generation of digital infrastructure, the "invisible backbone" already powering the world's largest industries, you could say we're all space professionals now.

Separating Fact from Science Fiction

Our market-leading position as investors isn't due simply to our depth of industry experience. It's a result of how we operate: our investment thesis and the discipline of our investment strategy. There's an art to evaluating new technologies and untested entrepreneurs in a rapidly evolving market. You need good data, sober analysis, and an effective decision-making process for drawing actionable signals from the noise.

The challenge of doing this is multiplied in a market as hot as today's Space Economy. The promise of easy money draws hucksters like blood does sharks. A glance at the crypto sector, where the negative fallout is more advanced, more visible, and therefore easier to understand from the outside, illustrates the consequences of a naïve approach in such an environment. Caution is advised.

In 2018, a company chaired by an eccentric billionaire with a sketchy track record announced its intention to launch humans to the Moon within two years. The cost? Ten thousand dollars a ticket. Considering the fact that you can pay three times that amount for a first-class ticket from Los Angeles to Dubai, the offer seemed a little too good to be true. Despite that fact and even though the company's CEO had no relevant experience, the company raised tens of millions of dollars from well-known Bay Area venture capitalists.

With a pile of capital and only two years until launch, you'd think the company would have prepared for take-off. But no. Instead, it threw money at expensive, life-sized mock-ups to tote around Washington and show off to government agencies in the hopes of raising even more funding for its scheme. Despite the complete lack of tangible progress toward the goal of a Lunar landing, people continued to be swept away by the vision.

Another founder said he would send ordinary people to Mars. Fill out an application, pay a fee, and you, too, might become one of the world's first crowd-sourced astronauts. That guy had no relevant experience, either. When he pitched me the concept, I asked him how he planned to actually get to Mars: "JFK didn't have a plan when he said we were going to the Moon," he replied.

To quote Tom Ingersoll once more: "Vision without execution is hallucination."

If you're going to invest in space, keep your head. Today is not the day for the more ambitious notions of the early Space Economy such as asteroid mining. The Emerging Industries of the Space Economy are coming sooner than many think. Still, before any of these advanced possibilities become commercial realities, we can expect to see a steady drumbeat of iteration and accomplishment—not just talk and flashy websites. (More on these Emerging Industries in Chapter 10.) In the meantime, real-world opportunities in the three satellite stacks of GPS, Geospatial Intelligence (GEOINT), and Satellite Communications (SatCom) come to fruition every day, mostly ignored by the space crazies even as they generate value for the kinds of investors who read the fine print and question every assumption.

In this chapter, I will show you how to zero in on space businesses with merit while steering clear of the boondoggles.

Picking the Right Horse: Evaluating Opportunities in the Space Economy

If you only read the latest breathless press releases from the handful of "hot" space companies who are vocal about their plans, you will end up with a wildly distorted perspective of what is currently feasible and what is still around the corner. A little hype goes a long way. In a hot market, it's essential to temper the hype with a broader perspective.

Today, there are more good, trustworthy sources of information about the Space Economy than ever before. A growing number of talented business journalists cover this territory with intelligence, rigor, and a relative lack of bias. This is by no means an exhaustive list, but here are some good sources of information on the business side of space: Michael Sheetz, Jeff Foust, Morgan Brennan, Loren Grush, Miriam Kramer, Joey Roulette, Ashlee Vance, Eric Berger, Marina Koren, Aria Alamalhodaei, Christian Davenport, Kenneth Chang, Jackie Wattles, Micah Maidenberg, and Tim Fernholz. If you want to understand the Space Economy, prioritize these thoughtful voices over the latest space "visionaries."

Ultimately, however, you must assemble your own picture to understand where growth is happening, why it's happening there, and what the ramifications of that growth might be. Start with what actually leaves the launchpad today, and then play the tape forward. This is Investing 101: If used car sales go up, demand will spike for tree-shaped air fresheners. SpaceX tipped the first domino by bringing launch costs down, but the real growth will happen due to the secondary and tertiary consequences of that shift. What are those consequences likely to be?

"The lowering of launch costs is the Gordian knot I've run at during my career," former NASA Deputy Administrator Lori Garver told me in May 2019, "and much more can still be done. Through reusability and competition, we will open markets that we can't currently imagine." For investors, it isn't about what was sold to a customer today but, rather, what that new thing will make possible tomorrow. As Wayne Gretsky famously advised, skate to where the puck is going.

"To me, the smart investments are in markets where we know the value from space will be unique," Garver said. "For example, with so many satellites in orbit, are they going to need to be refueled regularly? Are they going to need ongoing servicing and maintenance?" Just as the Interstate Highway System led to everything from motels to McDonald's, the building out of orbital infrastructure will spur demand for an array of complementary products and services. Apply a little imagination and you start to see possibilities.

"Invest across a broad array of space-centric activities," Garver said. "Communications has always been extremely profitable and important. Remote sensing. GPS. The fact is, there's never been this kind of opportunity with space, all because of driving down launch costs. We're just at the beginning."

In 2017, investor Justus Kilian found himself looking across the landscape for an area of technology with "planetary-scale" potential. That's when he realized that "space was an investable category."

"I'd lived in markets where a lack of communication and internet infrastructure was leaving entire generations behind, creating a digital divide," Kilian told me. "When cellular companies finally provided basic access, people quickly created brilliant, leapfrog solutions: mobile payment solutions, energy production through distributed grids. As phone costs came down, people in Kenya were using GPS to track wildlife on the Serengeti and creating homegrown Uber-like software to coordinate motorbike rickshaws."

To Kilian, there was a clear parallel between what had happened when cell service spread across Africa and what might happen as satellite constellations blanketed the skies: "Once I realized the potential of this truly global technology stack, I decided I wanted in." That decision brought Kilian to Space Capital as a Principal. Now, as a partner, he continues to be an essential part of the firm's value offering.

Operating partner Tom Whayne is another important ingredient in our secret sauce. In 2021, Maxar named Whayne its chief strategy officer. It was an obvious choice for the company. Whayne had been the lead strategic advisor to DigitalGlobe—which Maxar later acquired—for its 2013 acquisition of the GEOINT company GeoEye. Whayne had also led financing efforts for satellite constellations. And, as CFO of OneWeb from 2018 to 2021, Whayne had led that company's successful effort to raise more than $3 billion in capital. He had also managed OneWeb's 2020 sale process, which resulted in its acquisition by a consortium led by Bharti Global and the British government.

Whayne's shift to the Space Economy followed a successful career in investment banking at institutions like Credit Suisse First Boston and Morgan Stanley. Whayne saw the merits of investment banking, but he wanted to be where the real action was happening, even if few in his industry seemed to realize it.

"Space was still very much a niche market," he told me, "and there wasn't much in the way of venture activity at the investment banks." When fundraising deals did come together, they were handled as a sideline by bankers who specialized in telecoms, aerospace, and defense. "Now, most banks have people who work full-time on financings and strategic activity involving the space industry," Whayne said. "Technological and regulatory changes over the last ten years have significantly expanded the ecosystem."

Today, Bank of America, Morgan Stanley, and other large financial institutions are actively creating space investment vehicles and educating customers about these opportunities. Deloitte, McKinsey, and other consulting firms are also joining the fray. No serious player can afford to ignore this opportunity any longer. Unfortunately, many of the "experts" advising these large institutions about the Space Economy lack the networks, operational experience, and track record to offer trustworthy guidance.

Raising money for startups has gotten dramatically easier in Whayne's view: "There's a lot more excitement around space because of the SpaceX factor alone," he said. "It's huge. With launch costs coming down, it's opened up so many more use cases. From a geopolitical perspective, the Chinese saw Musk and got nervous: 'We have to invest in space for national security reasons. This guy is taking the industry to another level.' The impact isn't just on this country but on our closest strategic competitor."

Whayne has seen ripple effects from each of SpaceX's technological breakthroughs: first successful landing, first crewed launch, and so on. When SpaceX makes news, Whayne sees company creation, VC investment in the space sector, and space activity surge across the board. This is also true of governments, not only in the United States and China but worldwide: "Musk scares competitors, but he also scares governments."

When Whayne decided to focus his career on space, he did his homework: "A good banker learns from people who know the business better than they do," he said. "You listen, you learn, and you leverage off of people who have really thought about the critical technologies and commercial considerations that underscore their business plans. You engage in conversations with them and stress-test and perform sensitivity analyses."

The fact that Whayne spends significant time talking to people who know better makes him something of an outlier among his peers: "Most of the bankers out there take a management business plan, do the numbers, and that's it," he said. "A good banker learns from people who are close to the action. In the case of a satellite company that touches national security, for example, you're dealing with fairly sophisticated individuals on the board and in upper management, some with intelligence backgrounds. These people won't tell you anything explicitly. However, you can take cues from the concerns they're willing to express. If you pay attention, they will help you figure out what really matters."

Moving forward, Whayne believes the Space Economy will continue to be countercyclical. Space companies are not as high-risk as other cutting-edge tech investments. Many leading firms in the Space Economy are fairly resilient to changing market conditions because they are part of a value chain that provides critical data to governments and enterprises, which if anything ramp up spending on data in volatile times.

"The Space Economy is becoming a strategic communications backbone," Whayne said. "The use cases for SatCom and EO [Earth Observation] are only growing from the standpoint of governments, which is the traditional customer for that data. These budgets are increasing as a share of overall defense budgets around the world. As long as you have some exposure to government dollars, you can weather a downturn."

The commercial side of things, in contrast, offers more long-term upside to companies: "Commercial use cases continue to expand as costs come down," Whayne said. "We see one new application of space technology after another. For example, money is coming into the environmental sector due to the increasing need for efficient monitoring technologies that address greater regulatory scrutiny."

Whayne looks for businesses that take a "dual-customer approach: part-government, part-enterprise." It's a best-of-both-worlds strategy: "Companies that pursue a diversified market approach are going to be positioned very well," he said. "Things can get very cyclical for those that focus exclusively on enterprise customers. When your first customer is government, and you extend from there, you are well-positioned in any environment."

The best customer in the Space Economy, according to Whayne, is still the U.S. Department of Defense, "both from the standpoint of addressable market and, more important, the standpoint of technological innovation." Build something of value to "the most important customer in the world," and then, to drive long-term growth, extend into the enterprise market from there.

This was Whayne's strategy for OneWeb as its CFO, and it's Maxar's strategy today. "If a start-up is solely focused on enterprise customers, I get nervous," he said. "If they hedge by starting with government and moving to enterprise, it gets more interesting." Another advantage of having the government as a customer is that it allows government leaders to "be part of the conversation."

"Otherwise," Whayne said, "you're going to be left on the outside, not just in terms of money but also technology transfer."

Operating successfully in a nascent market requires domain awareness: "You've got to do due diligence," Whayne said. "You have to work to find the truth on the ground. If you're somebody like me, you've got a financial lens. Just as important, however, is a technical person you can trust. I lean on the technical people the most. If that person also has some knowledge of markets, that's ideal." As we saw in the previous chapter with the failures of Kistler and Beal Aerospace, "the people who run into trouble are the ones who are siloed and don't understand both sides."

In Whayne's view, you're looking for three attributes in a management team: First, a deep understanding of the technologies and the relevant technical issues. Second, a clear and realistic commercial strategy that will generate attractive, risk-adjusted returns. Third, the ability to communicate.

"Many entrepreneurs come up with interesting ideas but have a commercial or financial blind spot," Whayne said. "On the other hand, finance teams are often made up of accountant types with no strategic background. This gets them in trouble because they only look through the rearview mirror. Bean-counters know how to say no, but not how to say yes in a responsible way to strategic activities. Defense contractors are notorious for that kind of thinking."

Whayne considers a founding team with not only business and technical acumen but also the ability to communicate and collaborate the safest bet: "The most valuable thing is to connect everything. Forming teams and establishing good communication between teams isn't easy. You end up with the tyranny of the entrepreneur. Wherever the entrepreneur's background is has a way of bleeding out into the organization. The founder may be a visionary, but if they ignore the commercial side or the financial side or elbow those who do have that expertise out of the discussion, it creates problems."

Over the next few years, Whayne expects a dominant force to emerge in every category within the Space Economy: "There will be one player and five or six other companies that will either be consolidated or go bankrupt. One company in every area. Looking back, we got Google and Amazon out of the last internet craze. Lots of roadkill—but people did pretty well with Google and Amazon."

In short, a great deal of value will be created, but concentrated in one or two companies within each category. As the market proves out which of these emerging technologies have legs, consolidation will accelerate.

"The established players are trying to get to scale in order to ward off new entrants," Whayne said. "Meanwhile, the national security importance of the space sector is increasing. Money is going in that direction because of what's happening geopolitically. The innovation driven by all of this investment—in LEO [low-Earth orbit] constellations, for example—is critical from a national security perspective."

Defense, of course, is only one of several priorities driving investment.

"From a climate standpoint," Whayne said, "what other way do you have to monitor the truth on the ground? With any form of terrestrial monitoring, you have to ask, is the party doing the monitoring trustworthy? If somebody is monitoring emissions with terrestrial technologies in Russia, for example, can you believe the data? Not necessarily. But if you can monitor emissions from space in a way that is standardized around the world, yes, you can."

Whayne sees the three satellite stacks becoming an integral piece of global infrastructure, "not just from a communications standpoint but also in terms of processing and storage. Companies and individuals will increasingly be reliant on space infrastructure. The change will only accelerate."

***

Again, it's still early days. Very few companies in the Space Economy have gone public, and the options for individuals to invest in these opportunities are limited. For venture capitalists like us, getting in on seed-stage opportunities requires a lot of hard work—above all, the careful cultivation and monitoring of our professional network. When someone leaves a notable role to "start something new," you can bet we're paying attention. A seed-stage company is, as Justus Kilian pointed out, as much about the team as the prototype. The right people with the wrong idea will get to the next stage much more quickly than the wrong people with the right one.

We see it as our role to support aspiring founders before they've even decided whether to start a company or not. This support can take the form of one-on-one conversations, connections to industry experts and potential co-founders, or leads for first hires via Space Talent, our space career job board. We seek to develop relationships with entrepreneurs and add value long before there's anything in the cards for us.

Investing in the Space Economy offers massive potential ROI, but if you have the temperament and the skill set, why not launch a career within it and earn your equity that way? In the next chapter, I'll offer profiles of professionals and leaders across the Space Economy and their hard-earned advice about finding your way in and working your way up.

CHAPTER 8

Navigating Space Careers: Seizing the Opportunity of a Lifetime

L earning how markets form at Oxford's Saïd Business School taught me to see the potential in the Space Economy. It didn't take long before I was hooked on the idea of joining this exciting new world. Though I was actively following industry developments in the news, I was still just an interested bystander. From the outside looking in, I wondered whether there was even a place in the Space Economy for someone lacking a technical background as I did.

Without an obvious career path or role model, I knew I would need creativity to get my foot in the door. Where would I even begin? At the time, nontechnical opportunities in the Space Economy were essentially nonexistent. From my vantage point in 2012, there wasn't a way into the industry for a finance, economics, and business guy whose professional experience was in entrepreneurship and banking.

One of the nice things about being a student—even an adult MBA student—is that pros are more likely to spend time answering your questions. In search of an insider's perspective and wielding my student credentials like a press pass, I reached out for informational interviews with people across the budding Space Economy. To my surprise, I received an open and enthusiastic welcome. The resounding response from the pros was that, yes, the industry was full of technical folks, but it needed more business people to efficiently, effectively, and responsibly manage its growth. As it turned out, my business experience made me a unicorn. The Space Economy was so early in the S curve of innovation that most business-oriented professionals hadn't yet seen the potential in it. From the perspective of those working within the Space Economy, I could blaze a trail for myself there.

As I related in the Introduction, my first step to gain relevant experience was to do pro bono work for the Lunar robotics firm Astrobotic. Today, with the Space Economy on much firmer footing, there are many more paid, entry-level opportunities available. There is also more diversity in terms of the roles that are in demand. There is no longer a real need to work for free.

Just as space increasingly touches on every part of business, nearly every type of career touches the Space Economy. However, it can be unclear what space careers look like and how candidates land these roles. The competition is fierce. More people than ever want to work at these companies. How do you get noticed? What are managers really looking for?

Whether you're on the verge of completing your education and seeking your first full-time position, or you want to leave another industry for an exciting new direction as I did, there is a place for you in the Space Economy. On the other hand, you might be ready for a change within the industry. Perhaps you want to leave stodgy defense contractor work behind for the excitement of a scrappy startup. Or, having had your fill of entrepreneurial scrappiness, you might be ready to work for a large satellite manufacturer. It doesn't matter where you're coming from or where you're hoping to go. Through stories and advice from successful space professionals, this chapter will illuminate a path forward, touching on every aspect of career development within this dynamic and fast-moving environment.

Educational Paths into the Space Economy

"Getting into space work depends on where you are in your career," Space Capital partner Justus Kilian told me. "If you're still in university, there's a tremendous amount of opportunity to get plugged in, such as NASA challenges. Look for opportunities to work on hardware or software that are being built now. It helps to create a portfolio that shows you're curious and interested and can do stuff."

As Deputy Administrator of NASA under Barack Obama, Lori Garver played an important role in the evolution of the Space Economy. "I'm not an engineer or a scientist," Garver told me. "I have a political science and economics background. That's how I come at space." Today, she is senior fellow at Harvard Kennedy School's Belfer Center for Science and International Affairs and a member of the board of directors of Hydrosat. Garver is also the founder of Earthrise Alliance, a nonprofit using Earth Observation (EO) data to fight climate change, and co-founder of the Brooke Owens Fellowship, which offers paid internships and executive mentorship to women interested in aerospace.

Despite the lack of a traditional STEM background, Garver has led an influential career in the Space Economy. At NASA, she was head of policy under Bill Clinton, and she went on to work on space policy for both the John Kerry and Hilary Clinton campaigns. After Garver debated Barack Obama's space policy expert during the 2008 Democratic primary, the Obama team asked her to lead their transition team for NASA.

"Once I agreed," she said, "they asked me what I would be most interested in doing if I were to serve in the administration itself. My dad always counseled me to ask for something one step higher than I thought I could get. Since my dream job was Chief of Staff at NASA, I said, 'Deputy.'" To her surprise, Garver got the job.

The Brooke Owens Fellowship that Garver co-founded is an excellent example of the many different kinds of programs and opportunities available for talented young people interested in space.

"Our goal with the fellowship is to support a more diverse and thereby more innovative workforce for the space community," Garver said. "The program offers undergraduate women internships at commercial space firms. We also assign these students accomplished industry mentors. I'm so proud of the space community for supporting the initiative the way it has."

A spin-off of the Brooke Owens Fellowship is the Patti Grace Smith Fellowship, designed along similar lines and dedicated to creating a "meaningful, effective pathway into successful aerospace careers and future aerospace industry leadership to people whose race and ethnicity has made them the subject of systemic bias." As a teenager, Patti Grace Smith was a plaintiff in the landmark legal case that led to the integration of Alabama's schools. She went on to an illustrious career in space. Among her many roles and accomplishments, Smith ran the Office of Commercial Space Transportation for more than a decade, "overseeing the licensing of the first inland spaceport, the first private human spaceflight, and the first launches of Elon Musk's privately developed rocket, the SpaceX Falcon 1."[1]

Inevitably, higher education lags behind the sudden skill demands created by tech booms. As growth has continued across the Space Economy over the last few years, however, top educational institutions are starting to catch up. Harvard

Business School, for example, just launched a course, "Space: Public and Commercial Economics," believed to be the "first course on the economics of the space sector to be taught at an elite educational institution."[2] Matthew Weinzierl, the professor teaching the course, hopes it will "inspire other places to have their own offerings on space and make this something that is talked about at business schools more broadly."

This just scratches the surface. An online search reveals a growing array of educational programs; public and private prizes, grants, and internships; and other academic and industry opportunities intended to encourage and empower talented people who are interested in space. If you don't have the skills to contribute meaningfully to the Space Economy yet, go and get them.

The Right Stuff

Talking directly to leaders in the Space Economy, you discover that a shortage of talent is the biggest obstacle to growth today. A decade ago, space startups lured tech talent away from the likes of Apple and Google. Today, space companies are in a war for talent with each other.

The competition can be off the charts in the case of specialized skills like radio-frequency engineering, where the supply of engineers is still drastically below the demand. However, the talent gaps will close. A generation of academically gifted Millennial and younger workers are turning to space in search of more meaningful work than the moribund internet giants can offer. In parallel, older scientific and engineering talent, frustrated with the bureaucracy and stasis at large incumbents, are making late-career shifts for more dynamic opportunities.

This combination of demand for talent and pools of hidden talent led us to create a career platform, Space Talent, as a marketplace to connect companies in the Space Economy with the world's best employees. With 30,000 open roles and 700 companies as of this writing, Space Talent matches credible employers with top talent while providing insights into the ever-expanding range of opportunities. Even if you're not ready to start your job search in earnest, Space Talent is worth a look. You may be surprised by the breadth of roles and diversity of hiring organizations. Leveraging these opportunities, however, requires characteristics beyond any particular technical skill. Academic pedigree counts for something, but companies are far more interested in a demonstrated interest in space and a record of real-world accomplishments.

"I like to hire for capability," Rendered.ai founder and CEO Kundtz told me, "and a willingness to get things done. It helps to see evidence of being able to deliver." Don't wait for your first job to build a resume of accomplishment, either. "Even in college," Kundtz said, "there are ways to take academic projects beyond what might be required by the class. There are internships where you can contribute to a meaningful deliverable. Building a widget at an internship is a lesson in selling to an internal customer. It's an opportunity to learn more about the users of the things you're going to build."

Going beyond the technological challenge is key: "Demonstrating that you've taken the time to think about, 'Who's going to use this? What do they need?' is a differentiator for someone entering the field," Kundtz said. "You need to be sensitive not just to the merits of the product but to the needs of the customer. How will they use it? How can you help them? Customers don't buy products; they buy solutions. I try to hire 'solutioners.' It's usually easy to see evidence of that mentality early in a person's career."

If you already have technical skills, consider augmenting them with leadership, management, and communication training. For Space Economy managing partner Tom Ingersoll, getting a master's degree in engineering management involved taking several core MBA classes. Looking back,

Ingersoll believes that working at McDonnell Douglas without a business background would have gotten him "stuck doing the analysis or writing code." Instead, he was put to work on the bigger picture.

"I could manage projects because I understood budgets, schedules, management techniques, marketing, and how to work with customers," Ingersoll said. Engineering and other technical skills are critical, but if technical skills are all you bring to the table, it will limit your leadership potential. To work on the why, not just the how, consider a broader curriculum.

Since the field is changing so rapidly, it's okay if your degree doesn't align perfectly with your choice of career. You can compensate for that: "Getting involved in real-world projects as an intern or through another kind of program makes a huge difference when applying to companies like SpaceX for some of these highly coveted positions," Justus Kilian said. "You need to show capability way beyond academic performance."

"Regardless of your career stage," Kilian said, "start by educating yourself about the part of the industry you're interested in: geospatial, Internet of Things (IoT), space-based or terrestrial-based, and so on. Go where the community is gathering. Build your professional network. Follow your curiosity. Opportunity is everywhere. We're still in the early innings."

Choosing the Right Job

There are many different roles to play in the Space Economy. For many with a declared interest in space, however, the dream begins in the same way: "In high school," Violet Labs co-founder Lucy Hoag told me, "I decided I wanted to be an astronaut. I'd always been interested in uncharted territories and new frontiers. Obviously, space is the ultimate."

The desire to be an astronaut seems almost universal among thrill-seeking kids. Once you learn more about the different opportunities available, however, it becomes easier to see the paths that fit your unique strengths. These careers, though fascinating and rewarding, don't attract as many YouTube views as videos of astronauts drinking coffee in zero gravity, however. Before you commit yourself to your childhood ambition, do your research and explore the full spectrum of possibilities. It was at USC that Hoag realized that she was more interested in designing spacecraft than piloting them. She went on to earn her bachelor's, master's, and PhD in astronautical engineering.

Pursuing her doctorate at USC's Viterbi School of Engineering, Hoag worked on cutting-edge research into AI-based spacecraft design, creating an automated satellite design and optimization tool called Spider. This experience led her to DARPA, where Hoag was involved in programs like Phoenix, intended to harvest components from inactive satellites in geostationary orbit, and SeeMe, a disposable, low-Earth orbit (LEO) satellite constellation for sending EO imagery to soldiers on the battlefield. After DARPA, Hoag pivoted to consumer tech, doing stints at Google, Waymo, and then Lyft, where she worked on autonomous vehicles. "A self-driving car is basically a satellite on the ground," Hoag said. "A lot of the same sensor modalities and design principles. I had a ton of fun getting into that world." Through these disparate experiences, Hoag accumulated the knowledge, experience, and professional network she needed to successfully co-found a company.

Many factors come into play when deciding where to apply for jobs and which roles to accept, but people are an excellent compass. The Space Economy is still a small world. Relationships are paramount. Scrutinize potential colleagues at any prospective firm. Look closely at their qualifications and accomplishments. Salary and benefits matter, but never lose sight of career development. Go to the forefront whenever possible. In retrospect, would you have taken a management role at Beal Aerospace over an entry-level spot at SpaceX? Think about how much any given job will challenge you and help you learn. What will you experience there that you couldn't see anywhere else? How will the job expand your network? Even if it isn't ideal in every respect, will this opportunity lead to a better one down the road?

Tom Ingersoll's experience working on the Delta Clipper program at McDonnell Douglas was a highlight of his career because of what it taught him: "I worked with brilliant people," he said, "and now I see that many of the management philosophies that I've developed came from that project. I learned what it meant to actually fly hardware and what the hallmarks of success are. I did this by working with great people, understanding the value great people bring to a team, and seeing individuals come together on a project to accomplish extraordinary things. That was a huge step for me."

For Ingersoll, the job itself held little appeal at first: "I just wanted to work with the smartest people," he said. "I wasn't that excited about aerospace, and I wasn't that excited about Southern California, but they were clearly the smartest people and I wanted to figure out where I stacked up."

It can be difficult to gauge just how interesting or exciting a job will be when you're on the outside looking in. An opportunity at a company that's brimming with talent merits close consideration even if the job itself doesn't sound exciting on the surface. Those employees probably know something you don't.

In Defense of Defense Contractors

Looking for a way into the Space Economy, keep the entire ecosystem in mind. While the on-tap kombucha might be fresher at a startup, there are many good reasons to consider working for a large, established company. Even defense contractor work can teach valuable lessons.

"I had several opportunities to leave McDonnell Douglas," Tom Ingersoll told me. "But I'm glad I stuck it out for the scaling experience alone. I put together billion-dollar budgets and managed teams of five or six hundred people. It taught me the challenges involved in scaling and honed my management approach. Scaling, especially for someone who wants to be an entrepreneur, is critical. Sticking around was a great choice for me and made a significant difference in my career."

If you have entrepreneurial ambitions, it's worth considering a stint in government despite the bureaucracy and delay: "You can be an entrepreneur in any job, and NASA is a great place to do it," Planet Labs co-founder Robbie Schingler said. "I worked on a number of really fun projects during my career there." Named special assistant to the director of the Ames Research Center and eventually Chief of Staff to the Chief Technologist, Schingler helped incubate NASA's Space Technology program.

"In retrospect, NASA trained me to be an entrepreneur of a VC-funded company," Schingler said. "That's mostly thanks to 7120.5D, the NASA Office of Chief Engineer Program Management guidelines. Every step of a project, you have a design review, where the project is assessed against progress on technology development, management, and cost of the program, all while making sure you're still hitting your science metrics."

"Each time you did a review, you got a new slug of money," Schingler said. "You keep building your technology, validating your science hypotheses, building out your team, all while ensuring you're actually on cost and on budget. When we left to start Planet Labs and decided to do it with venture capital, it turned out it was the same thing. Can you build the team? Can you validate your market hypotheses? Can you build a technology? Do you have a moat? Do you have a differentiator? It's all the same stuff. NASA teaches entrepreneurship."

Climbing the Ladder to Leadership

In a period of rapid growth, the incentives to switch jobs can be hard to resist. When the competition for talent is fierce, compensation packages become highly aggressive. No doubt there is a financial upside in playing leapfrog from one company to the next at times like this. That said, try to prioritize your long-term professional development. Doing the same job somewhere else for more money is appealing. Still, it can make better sense to stay in your current role long enough to stack up concrete accomplishments and earn greater levels of responsibility.

External conditions, on the other hand, can be a very good reason to move on, even if you're comfortable where you are. You can't afford to ignore the winds of change. Tom Ingersoll heard those winds blowing at McDonnell Douglas after it merged with Boeing. "My wife and I had four little kids," Ingersoll said. "I had a house payment, not a lot of savings, and I was on the fast track at McDonnell Douglas. But I quit my job to go work for a startup." Ingersoll had learned a lot at McDonnell Douglas, but he knew that the Space Economy was at an inflection point. It was time to go: "Do your homework, be prepared, but also be willing to take a calculated risk when an opportunity comes your way."

At Skybox Imaging, Dirk Robinson played a key role in the development of Skybox's revolutionary imaging satellite constellation, an engineering feat that posed many challenges. Later on, at Google, Robinson led the team that expanded the Google Maps platform. He attributes his success as a leader in part to his education, less because of his classes than his extracurriculars. "In school, I was lucky enough to stumble into leadership roles in various associations and communities," he said. "Without knowing it at the time, I was learning how to communicate and coordinate across groups. I was learning how to make plans, bring people together, and get things done."

In graduate school, Robinson learned another important leadership skill: flexibility. Leading a diverse team demands it. "I had the opportunity to work closely with engineers and professors from all around the world," he said. "That gave me a window into the different experiences, cultures, and values that people bring to work. These days, most of us are working with, selling to, or buying from across the globe. Those experiences early in my career taught me how to build partnerships and get things done in the diverse world we operate in."

The Skills in Demand

"When most people think of space, they think rockets," Justus Kilian said. "Up until now, that has been the area of great opportunity. There has probably been 100x growth in launch over the last five years. Demand for propulsion engineers, for example, has been fierce. In fact, all the high-level propulsion engineers have been building engines across the big producers for a decade or two." However, the areas of demand will change as the Space Economy evolves.

"The single greatest position in demand across our ecosystem is the software engineer," Kilian said. "Software optimizes hardware, so these engineers play a crucial role. They're building more efficient supply chains. They're creating more powerful business intelligence tools. For example, many of the systems used at SpaceX internally are proprietary solutions developed by its software engineers."

"Data science roles are also very competitive right now," Kilian said. "Data decides success. For example, telemetry projections guide each rocket. If the projections fail, so does the launch. So these software roles demand serious competence."

"It's the interface between software and the mechanical devices that are servicing people where I see opportunity," Tom Ingersoll said. "We can't go to space on software, so you need an interface. You can't build a driverless car on just software. You still need the hardware." Along these lines, Tom sees great potential in the multidisciplinary field of mechatronics, a specialty concerned with integrating computing, electromechanical systems, robotics, and automation. Everything from IoT devices to avionics to biomechatronics—powered exoskeletons—falls under the mechatronic purview. As you might imagine, there is a growing demand for people with mechatronic backgrounds across the Space Economy.

Other areas of demand include software development that touches on AI and machine learning and nearly every engineering subspecialty. However, if your skills lie elsewhere—from graphic design to publicity—forego getting a technical graduate degree until you've explored the opportunities that might already be waiting for you.

"If you're mid-career," Kilian said, "backgrounds in communication, traditional tech, logistics, image processing and cloud capabilities, and many other skill sets—technical-, business-, or legal-oriented—have a home in the Space Economy."

Pivot Toward Learning

In addition to being an operating partner at Space Capital and a mentor with Techstars, Aaron Zeeb is a leader at Safire Partners, an executive search firm in Southern California focused on emerging growth companies. Zeeb wanted to work in tech but didn't see himself as an engineer. Instead, he got his start recruiting for large telecoms. This gave him crucial tech industry experience and a glimpse at the inner workings of the "hardcore infrastructure projects that were the backbone of the internet."

When the dot-com bust brought the first large wave of internet-related hiring to a standstill, Zeeb pivoted to aerospace, where he recruited for contractors like Lockheed Martin and Bell Helicopter. One of the benefits of trying different career paths and industries is discovering where you don't belong: "I remember walking through the halls of some of these companies," he recalled. "Some of these were top-secret projects. Buildings with no windows. Ten-foot-high cubicles so you couldn't see other people's computer screens. Executive offices around the perimeter. It was just very awkward, very uninspiring, and very drab."

For all the frustrations involved in working with legacy organizations, aerospace clients gave Zeeb recruiting experience that would prove crucial later in his career at SpaceX and beyond, as well as a rare window into the philosophy and mindset of the large incumbents where much of the foundational work in technology still happens.

Given the option, steer toward the roles that offer greater learning potential. When you run into an obstacle like an unexpected layoff, take the opportunity to move toward discomfort and growth. Cross-pollination drives progress. Nothing beats a resume packed with a breadth of unique experiences. There's only so much you can learn from any single vantage point.

Skybox's Dirk Robinson points to curiosity as his career superpower. "My curiosity drives me to reach out, make connections, and learn about aspects of the systems, business, and organization falling outside my primary domain," Robinson said. "I often spend time with people who are not normally part of my day-to-day, such as customers, legal teams, finance, and HR. I have found that doing so gives me a clearer picture of the systems we all operate within. This in turn helps me identify opportunities and 'see around the corner,' so to speak." The importance of curiosity to your career can't be overstated.

"I am a naturally curious person," Robinson said. "I love to learn. Looking back, this curiosity has served me well in two ways. First, when making career decisions, I prioritize working with people from whom I can learn. This has meant getting to work with world-class machine learning researchers like Peter Hart and David Stork, who literally wrote the book on machine learning used in grad schools across the world; with an amazingly sharp team of entrepreneurial engineers at Skybox Imaging; and with executive leaders like Joe Rothenberg, Tom Ingersoll, and Camie Hackson, people who really know how to build and run large, high-performing engineering organizations. Working with people I admire has taught me useful skills and inspired me to do my best."

Space Capital's Justus Kilian followed his curiosity from a career in finance. As a senior financial analyst at Merrill Lynch, Kilian noticed a trend: "It wasn't just the standard world of venture capital, where the part-time financier raised and deployed capital," he told me. "It was the operator-centric model that said, 'Hey, I know how to build this. I can empathize with you, the founder, because I've done it, too.' The operator-centric funds were the ones raising all the money." Intrigued, Kilian spent the next five years of his career acquiring operational experience himself: investing across south Asia and east Africa and helping portfolio companies build their sales functions, restructure their balance sheets, and develop management training programs, to name a few areas of focus. Kilian even spent a year as an interim CFO and operations manager in northern Uganda to help a priority investment achieve high growth.

"This experience gave me new insights into what investors want and where opportunity could be found in a market," Kilian said, "as well as plenty of tactical knowledge about building and operating different kinds of businesses that actually create shareholder value and return capital to investors."

"I came out of Harvard in 2005 with bachelor's and master's degrees in applied math and statistics," Arbol founder Siddhartha Jha told me. "My career began in quantitative analysis. Figuring out how markets work on a very fundamental level. In fact, I spent the first five years of my career working with interest rates. Interest rates are a very good foundation for understanding how all financial markets work. At their core, most markets are a reflection of interest rates. Understanding interest rates helps you understand public stock markets, commodities, venture capital, and many of the broader trends in the economy at any given time."

No career advisor would tell a young person interested in the Space Economy to study interest rates. Yet, Jha's curiosity about interest rates led him toward one of the most promising near-term applications of Geospatial Intelligence (GEOINT) data: parametric insurance. In other words, if Jha hadn't followed his interests, he would never have founded Arbol.

"My first love was always commodities," Jha said. "Ships, pipelines, the basic materials that drive our day-to-day lives. How does food make it to our tables? How does gas flow into our cars? That's why I left J.P. Morgan to join a startup hedge fund. I was really focused on understanding markets: oil and gas, corn and soybeans, copper and lead, cattle, hogs, you name it. If it's even reasonably liquid, I've analyzed and traded it in the commodity space. Those experiences gave me a very good overview of how different markets work from a production, consumption, and logistics standpoint—and how they interact with each other."

Jha learned about the potential of commercial EO satellites working in quantitative analysis: "Increasingly, you had satellites appearing in new applications. One application was the use of infrared satellites to assess crop health. I traded a lot of wheat and corn. In much of the world, official government data isn't reliable, and sending people in on the ground is impractical. You needed a practical and efficient way to measure the relative state of, say, the wheat crop in Argentina versus the one in Ukraine. Satellites offered an objective way to do that. So I became familiar with the potential from that standpoint. I also advised a group trying to launch one of the first commercial radar satellites. Both experiences taught me a lot about the satellite industry. When we started building out Arbol's infrastructure, we knew that satellite-based weather and vegetation data would be key."

One important takeaway from all this is that you can never afford to rest on your laurels when operating with cutting-edge technology. Keep one eye on your job and the other on the horizon.

"Every five or six years of my career," Aaron Zeeb said, "I've tried to take a step back, look at where things are going, and reevaluate." When it became clear that Silicon Valley had rebounded, Zeeb headed west, joining Google during its first big hiring spree. Talk about good timing. However, it wasn't luck but strategy that got Zeeb to Google at the right moment.

"Look at where the industry is going," Zeeb said, "and associate your career with those things." As the infrastructure layer of the internet was being built, Zeeb worked with telecoms. Once the internet's application layer took the forefront, Zeeb positioned himself at Google. In retrospect, Zeeb's decision to join SpaceX before the launch of its first rocket seems prescient. According to Zeeb, however, navigating tech is just a matter of paying attention and "staying ahead of where the industry is going." This raises the question: where does Zeeb see it going next?

"Launch is the sexy thing," Zeeb said, "but at the end of the day, rockets will be the UPS and FedEx trucks of the industry." The real action lies in leveraging the data from that orbital tech. "It's the Applications layer of the data, the intelligence of satellite systems, the sensor technology—that's where I would focus my career," he said. "If I were starting from scratch, these are the types of companies that I would gravitate towards."

"Engineering will always be a promising career opportunity," Dirk Robinson told me. "Engineering is a critical driver of human productivity, the most valuable resource on the planet. That is not to say that engineering careers will always be stable or static. The trends of software and automation will affect engineering careers as much as any other. However, there will always be a need for people with a strong fundamental understanding of the basic sciences as well as engineering principles: design, analysis, and testing. In my opinion, the most exciting engineering career opportunities in the coming years and decades will be in those fields that are transitioning from basic science into engineering: bio-engineering, neural interfaces, environmental engineering, sociological engineering, and quantum computing."

The Importance of Relationships

One of the most important relationships to seek out in any career is the right mentor: "Seek out mentors and become a mentor to others," Dirk Robinson said. "If you look for them, you will always be able to find mentors willing to help you in your career. A mentor is an incredibly valuable resource to help you understand and pursue your goals. They can help you identify the problems you want to solve and provide encouragement and motivation to move forward. Every successful person I know has mentors in their life."

"You look at pretty much anybody who's been successful and you'll find that somebody stepped in and helped them get to where they are," Tom Ingersoll said. "They vetted them and provided a level of credibility that gave them access." In Ingersoll's case, Pete Conrad, the astronaut who commanded the Apollo 12 mission, served as just such a mentor when they worked together at McDonnell Douglas. "Pete helped me immensely in my career," Ingersoll said.

Likewise, if you find yourself in a position to become a mentor, go for it: "Mentoring others will benefit you, even as you help others," Robinson told me. "Mentoring is a skill that can be learned and improved over time with practice. I have found it to be an incredibly rewarding experience, providing an opportunity to learn about patterns of success and failure that you can bring into your own life and career. It also makes a real impact on those you mentor."

At the end of the day, the best jobs still come through personal relationships. Reputation matters, not only once you're in charge but from the very start of your career. "You come out of college and think you know a lot, and you really know nothing," Ingersoll said. "You've got to pay your dues to learn your industry. You also need to build a network of people that you respect and, conversely, that respect you. They want someone who's going to listen, who's got talent, who's got drive, who's going to work, who's honest, who's got integrity. Make sure you put in the time to learn your craft and be the kind of person that people want to work with." This is true of any industry, but especially true of the nascent, high-stakes, high-growth Space Economy.

"You hire people because of what they know, you fire people because of who they are," Ingersoll said. "Are you the kind of person that really sharp people are going to want to work with? Are you kind? Are you respectful? Do you have positive energy? Are you a contributor? Those things aren't necessarily taught in school, but they have a huge impact on your ability to be successful in any kind of work environment."

***

Building a career in the Space Economy is just the beginning. As you move up the ladder, the challenge shifts to finding, hiring, and retaining other talented people to help achieve the company's vision.

As we've seen, there is a war for talent in the Space Economy. In the next chapter, I will share tactics and techniques organizations can use to win that war from leaders across industries. You can't achieve your own potential if you're not surrounded by the right team.

CHAPTER 9

Winning the War for Talent: A Guide to Recruiting and Retaining "The Right Stuff"

A war for talent rages in the Space Economy. A decade ago, companies like SpaceX had to lure software engineers away from Google and Facebook and avionics engineers from NASA and large defense contractors. Today, the talent war continues much closer to home, as cutting-edge startups within the Space Economy battle each other for the world-class employees they need to make their ambitious visions soar.

"Attracting talent isn't as easy as it was early on," Planet Labs CEO Robbie Schingler told me. "There's more competition. Rising interest in things like self-driving cars, robotics companies, green tech. Also, many companies in the space sector have raised a whole bunch of money. That's inflating salaries quite a bit. Simultaneously, there's been a shift in people not wanting to live in major cities anymore. When you're building hardware, you still need your team in the lab."

Just how hard has it become for companies to fill roles and keep them filled? One indication is in the rising number of acquisitions that don't make sense as acquisitions per se. Many are "acqui-hires," a common practice in tech. In acquisitions like these, the company's revenue stream, intellectual property, and customer base don't fully account for the sale price. Instead, the real target of the acquisition is the pre-assembled team of experts that comes bundled with the other assets of the organization. Acqui-hires often mean promising technologies and business models are abandoned as the acquirer—typically, an established incumbent—uses those new employees to fill pressing gaps in its existing business.

Another indication of the demand for talent in the Space Economy is the amount of poaching. Recruiters play hardball. Rising churn is a pressing problem for the Space Economy because complex, long-term projects are handed off repeatedly—never a good recipe for seeing them to a successful conclusion.

On the bright side, demand spurs supply. The core skills of the Space Economy, from mechatronics to machine learning, are being learned by larger and larger cohorts of students. In June of every year, an even-larger wave of graduates with the "right stuff" enters the workforce. Who will snatch them up first?

Assembling the Founding Team

We first discussed the challenge of finding the right co-founders in Chapter 5. The founding team plays an outsized role in the future direction of an organization. As Tom Whayne said about entrepreneurs in Chapter 7, "whatever their background is has a way of bleeding out into the organization." This can be a good or a bad thing depending on the background in question.

When it comes to assembling a founding team, your options are limited by economics: "There are only so many people in the world who have the training and capabilities to start a company," Rendered.ai CEO Nathan Kundtz told me. "Among those, even fewer can also work without significant income for an unknown period of time for an unknown return. That whittles the field." That said, it's still necessary to be very selective in forming early alliances.

"Bringing in people with impressive resumes sends a signal," Kundtz said, "reinforcing the kind of talent you want." However, there's more to being right for the founding team than academic pedigree. "What you really want are people who are willing to do the work," Kundtz said. "People who will sit at the computer and code. People who will pick up the phone and dial around and set up meetings and get things done. Starting a company successfully is all about momentum. It's never just finding the person who is the very best in a certain field. That person may not want to put the work in. They may have other things going on. You want talented people who are also going to get the ball rolling. Once you're headed in the right direction, you can always bring in specialized talent as needed."

In the Space Economy, founders still tend to come from a technical background, often boasting at least one related PhD. There's a reason for this, according to Kundtz. "In other fields," he said, "it's more common to find people who just left Harvard Business School with an MBA and are ready to start a company. That's harder to do in the Space Economy. Having a technical background is important to early sales because you need to be able to speak the language of the customer. Here, the customer is almost always deeply technical themselves. It's hard for people who don't know the language to enter these conversations credibly." Not everyone on a founding team needs a PhD in aerospace engineering, but at least one founding member should be able to speak the language of your customers, whomever they happen to be.

"Otherwise," Kundtz added, "people will write you off."

None of this means you need an academic background as robust as the one Nathan Kundtz has to found a company in the Space Economy. The entrepreneurs we invest in have followed many different paths. More important, think carefully about the skills and experiences *you* bring to the table and seek out co-founders who will complement your strengths.

From Founding Team to First Hires

Once your startup has momentum, it's time to bring in your first hires, the employees who will "establish the infrastructure, best practices, and culture of the organization," according to Kundtz. These early hires will have long-term ramifications for the trajectory of your company, so be strategic.

"If new technology is your focus," he said, "your first hire might be a brilliant Head of Product with deep domain expertise. If it's more of a business model innovation you offer, it might be a head of Business Development with a terrific network to grow your client list."

Organizational experience plays a key role at this stage. Decisions made by early hires will steer the structure, culture, philosophy, and approach of the company you're building. Select for track record, even if that means there's some duplication of skills with members of your founding team. "Even if you have someone brilliant on the founding team who already has the crucial technical expertise," Kundtz said, "you may still want a veteran VP of engineering with the experience to say, 'This is how an engineering team ought to be structured.'"

"From day one, I was very focused on hiring for the complexity of this endeavor," Arbol founder Siddhartha Jha said. "Arbol touches on data and technology on the one side and regulatory, legal, insurance, and financial issues on the other. So it requires many different types of expertise. No one could possess it all. My job is to make sure that the two worlds bridge well, that the firm integrates the new and the old. Arbol is not a pure tech company. It's infused with technology, but it needs to fit into the world of regulations, insurance, derivatives, and securities. We need to know all the rules and operate in unison. Arbol is succeeding because all these different kinds of expertise work together as one team."

"We are laser-focused on hire, hire, hire," Lucy Hoag, co-founder of Violet Labs, told me. "The need for our product is growing. We want to get it to market quickly so that our customers can have a better experience now."

Now that Violet Labs has raised its first round of capital, the founders are rapidly building the team, beginning with software engineering to jumpstart progress on the product and with essentials like product management, quality assurance, and business development to follow. The co-founders understand that the mindset of these early hires will establish the culture of the organization: "We're looking to hire folks that are equally passionate about what we're doing and want to be in a forward-thinking and—hopefully—really fun team."

Violet Labs, like many startups across industries today, is remote-first. "It's an important decision for us and was certainly influenced by our experiences during COVID building a spacecraft while scattered all over the country," Hoag said. Remote work during the pandemic proved to Hoag and her co-founder, Caitlin Curtis, that this approach was not just feasible but in fact a path to superior results: "We each saw how doing the job remotely cut down on the noise—the logistics and mechanics—involved in being in-person."

"At Lyft," Hoag said, "people were able to work remotely as much as they pleased when COVID hit. I saw how that affected the quality of their work as well as their overall happiness and well-being. We want to champion that in our company." Building a remote-first company from the ground up does pose unique challenges, however. Unlike Lyft, Violet Labs must establish its company culture primarily over the internet. "We want a strong team culture with camaraderie and trust. For communication, we rely on tools like Slack and Notion. We also hold periodic in-person retreats to tackle the IRL [in real life] part."

One of the interesting aspects of hiring at Violet Labs has been the chasm between two very different industries: "The Venn diagram of people who have built things like space-craft, self-driving cars, and drones and people who have built fantastic web apps, it's essentially two separate circles. Very little overlap." What Hoag and Curtis have found, however, is that the mission of Violet Labs is their most effective recruiter. "Software developers are extraordinarily excited about working in this industry," she said, "building something that will affect the development of something like a rocket. It's a chance to rev-olutionize a stagnating part of this industry, and people see that as vitally important."

As we've seen, one of the key advantages of hiring top talent in the Space Economy is the shared sense of mission. "People want to work in the Space Economy just to work in the Space Economy," Nathan Kundtz said. "If we were building missiles, we'd have to pull from a very different pool of talent. The impor-tant work that we're doing absolutely helps with recruiting. It matters that we're on the cutting edge of something that looks like it's going to explode with capital formation. It's obviously a good idea to fish here."

Where to Find Talent

Top organizations invest in internship programs. Since the work being done by many of the most exciting companies in the industry remains opaque to outsiders, getting college students into the lab, office, or hangar is the fastest way to communicate what is most compelling about what is being built.

Unlike highly competitive arenas like finance and Big Tech, the Space Economy offers a meaningful mission above and beyond profit. Millennial, Gen Z, and younger employees prioritize purpose and company mission more than older generations do. An audacious goal with the potential for genuine impact on global issues like climate, sustainability, access to connectivity, and a secure food supply carries weight. Younger people want to do more than gamify customer attention spans and capture eyeballs. Convincing them to join your organization, however, requires that you articulate a coherent vision for your company. You have to be able to communicate your values and long-term intentions authentically. It isn't enough to highlight the gee-whiz aspects of a new gizmo. To win the war for talent, convince people why your mission matters.

"You can't just throw 'space' in the company name and expect that to do the recruiting work for you," Space Capital partner Justus Kilian told me. "It feels like literally every space company is called 'space something,' and that's simply not enough. You have to articulate a very clear vision of what you want to achieve and how you're going to get there."

The right vision is paramount: "Some of the biggest, most complicated, and most challenging problems we face are global in scale," Kilian said. "Climate change, global connectivity and the digital divide, and agriculture and food production are great examples. The best employees want to take on the toughest problems—technically challenging as well as meaningful. Another social media app just doesn't have the gravity of tackling climate change. That's where space companies can differentiate themselves. They have a global mission. They're trying to solve big, important problems. People can see a real impact as a consequence of their day-to-day work. Space companies compete with Google and Facebook based on big, technical breakthroughs and doing work that actually matters."

Conveying this to potential hires is an art: "It all starts with how you articulate what your brand is and why people should join you on this crazy journey," Kilian said. "SpaceX does a great job of that. Their stated goal is to make humanity a multiplanetary species, and that begins with sending people to Mars. Ultimately, everything they do is in service of that mission."

Young employees bring energy, enthusiasm, and cutting-edge technical skills. For other assets, such as real-world experience, look to industry veterans. Valuable knowledge in areas like avionics, rocketry, and older programming languages is concentrated among older employees.

On the bright side, people with decades of experience in relevant technological areas are out there. Thanks to the ageism prevalent in tech, however, they remain a somewhat untapped resource. Those still working are often eager to leave bureaucratic defense contractor work and the like behind for exciting startup opportunities. Others are in forced early retirement, squeezed out of the industry before its resurgence. When hiring for key skills, consider people with gaps in their resumes when they have the skills you need most.

Recruiting the Best

"We're hiring some PhDs," Anna Volkova, founder of Regrow, told me. "In those cases, I dig into *why* they wanted a doctorate. In some cases, they wanted to come to Australia and were just looking for a way to do it. When someone from Australia is doing their PhD, on the other hand, you know they have a different motivation. Before hiring them, I want to know whether the candidate is academically minded, industry minded, or commercially minded."

Understanding the motivation of prospective hires matters in an arena where passion plays an important role. "One of the secret ingredients is a purpose," Volkova said. "Are you doing this because you want to advance humanity's knowledge? Or are you doing it because there's a problem you want to fix? Do you want to make an impact? What drives you?"

"Personally," Volkova said, "I was always driven by what actually moves and shakes the market, what makes an impact. Not just by academia, not by figuring out the edge of innovation that you can reach. To me, it was important that it was applied. I look at innovation from that perspective. Is there an end user? Am I doing this for someone who will use this today or tomorrow? People say that Millennials are hooked on impact. They want to see that they've become part of something bigger. I think more PhDs should open up their minds to that."

Aaron Zeeb of Safire Partners, whom we met in the previous chapter, has accumulated more than 20 years of experience in recruiting, working for companies ranging from Google, which went from 8,000 to 16,000 employees during his tenure, to SpaceX, where he spent six years helping the company grow from 300 employees to over 4,000. If you want to understand how to recruit top talent in a highly competitive landscape during a period of extraordinary growth, heed Zeeb's advice.

When tech began to rebound after the dot-com bust, Zeeb left the stodgy world of defense contractors behind to work for Google, which had gone public two years prior and was one year away from being ranked first on the *Fortune* "100 Best Companies to Work For" list.

"This was when Google redefined employee perks for tech companies," Zeeb said, "all in the name of attracting the best engineers." The perks were only part of Google's appeal, however. "They really defined themselves on the strength of their culture, and it was a great work environment, awesome to see from the inside. The strength of their programs. The strength of that brand. At the time, we were getting a resume every 1.2 seconds. It was insane."

Like Larry Page and Sergey Brin, Zeeb believes that world-class talent is the secret to scale. The secret to recruiting world-class talent, in Zeeb's opinion, is an inspiring vision that resonates with driven, ambitious individuals. Top performers respond to a challenge, and they like to work around other top performers who feel similarly inspired.

"You need to be competitive on benefits and amenities," Zeeb said, "but that's more about creating an environment where people can be successful. To attract the best talent, create an inspiring mission. You don't want people who are there for the free food. You want people who are inspired to achieve something incredibly difficult and important *and* whose eyes are wide open. Diversity of thought and perspective is important, but at the end of the day, people want to work with other people who are aligned towards the same mission and excited by that challenge."

For founders scaling into the stratosphere, doing this consistently requires a structured hiring process. An informal evaluation process that works well for a small team will break down once the pace accelerates. Google only maintained its standards as it scaled by building a "recruiting machine," according to Zeeb, and "optimizing every inch of it."

"Six months before I joined, they were doing fourteen interviews per candidate," he said. "After collecting and analyzing all the interview data and linking that data to job performance, they realized that using a structured format and evaluating the right criteria gave them enough data to make an informed decision after just four interviews. You're never going to get to hundred-percent informed, but four interviews could give you 90 percent confidence, while fourteen might get you to 92 percent."

Google taught Zeeb the importance of experimenting and optimizing when developing a hiring workflow. Google's rigid hiring practices aren't appropriate for every organization, but he believes every hiring process should be revised based on the results. Instead of copying Google or any other company, use your own data to refine a process until it works well for your needs.

"Every environment is unique," Zeeb said, "so their recruiting processes should be unique to them. The critical factor is making the process measurable and repeatable at scale, as well as reflective of the culture you're trying to create and the talent you're trying to attract."

Later on, at SpaceX, Elon Musk told Zeeb: "Process can become a substitute for thinking." The pace of a startup's growth may require a highly regimented and structured approach to hiring. Still, remain flexible and open-minded, particularly when filling instrumental roles. It was the tedium of Google's strict hiring process that left Zeeb open to other opportunities himself. Though SpaceX had yet to launch its first rocket when the company approached him about recruiting for them, Zeeb was quickly hooked by a look at its operations.

"Small teams of people, super-scrappy, super-iterative," he recalled. "The factory was right next to the engineering office. Everything was fully integrated. My perception of aerospace was Lockheed Martin, Bell Helicopter, eighty-foot cubicles, slow pace, drab offices, no windows. I could see immediately, even with that little dose of experience that I got earlier in my career, why SpaceX was different."

Originally, Musk founded SpaceX in Los Angeles because it had the highest concentration of aerospace talent. Now, Musk wanted Zeeb to recruit from farther afield. He wanted to inject the company with new ideas and ways of thinking. That meant recruiting from outside the traditional space industry. "We have the critical mass of aerospace talent," Musk told Zeeb. "My goal is not to be the next big aerospace contractor. We need to diversify. We need to get more people thinking about the space industry who aren't currently thinking about the space industry." At the time, the best tech talent was at companies like Google and Amazon. Musk wanted Zeeb to recruit them: "The whole goal was to bring people from Google and those types of companies into SpaceX, to get them to consider space as a career."

Zeeb's experiences at Google and SpaceX offer a powerful lesson in contrasts. Both companies succeed at recruiting the best and brightest, but in different ways. "Google had an amazing talent attraction process," Zeeb said. "They had these hiring committees. Before anyone got hired, the committee, comprised of some of the hirers and some of the best engineers, would sit down and collectively review the applicants. It was heavily focused on academics."

In contrast, "Musk was less concerned about academic pedigree. His major metric was 'evidence of exceptional ability.' And that can come in all forms. It can be where you went to school and how you did at school, but that's only a piece of it. More likely, it can be where you got hands-on experience, how you applied that experience, and whether that was self-initiated."

After working with two major companies during periods of rapid growth, Zeeb decided to focus on helping early-stage companies build a "foundation of talent." Together with his partner at Safire, Todd Gitlin, Zeeb helps venture-backed start-ups recruit executive talent. "It's a little challenging at those stages," he told me. "A lot of times you've got first-time founders. You're educating them. We spend a lot of time helping them think through how to hire the right founding team. Those first ten engineers lay the foundation of these companies."

While excellent organizations succeed in different ways, there are always common elements in the ones that attract the world's best: "All talented people not only want to be challenged but *need* to be challenged," Zeeb said. "They just don't do well at treading water. They need people to really push them." The pace is set from the top.

"I think there are very few entrepreneurs on the planet who will push you as hard as Elon Musk will push you," Zeeb said. "It's not for everyone."

The Right Culture Retains the Right Employees

"SpaceX has been able to keep as many employees as they have for as long as they have for a couple reasons," Justus Kilian told me. "One, they give their employees options so they're invested in the company. Two, they offer liquidity. People can see the value of staying. A lot of companies fail to communicate the value in their equity. In macro conditions like we see now, where valuations are changing and companies are raising flat or down rounds, options go underwater. They have no value. Companies lose great people when they don't account for that."

Financial incentives matter. Money alone, however, has the effect of retaining everyone, regardless of whether they're a good fit, let alone the best for the job. The right culture can shape an organization more powerfully than any compensation package. "In the early days of SpaceX, we had a lot of people from traditional aerospace companies," Aaron Zeeb told me, "and they were used to getting every other Friday off and not working sixty or eighty hours a week. At that time, we thought things would eventually calm down: 'Just wait, eighteen more months,' we'd say. 'Once we get Falcon 1 to orbit. Once we get Falcon 9 to orbit. Once we get Dragon. At the next milestone, things will return to normal.'" This ongoing struggle to manage employee frustrations only deferred the inevitable. "The reality was, we wanted to do something incredibly hard but also incredibly rewarding," Zeeb said. "So Elon's message became: SpaceX is the Special Forces. We do the job that others consider impossible. We operate in small teams. We give you a lot of responsibility. We iterate and move quickly. We will constantly challenge you, but we will do hugely impactful things."

This clarification of the ethos worked: "Once we changed the message, the culture of the company shifted," Zeeb said.

"The people who were used to the old way of doing things self-selected out. The rest committed to the mission one-hundred percent. The people who have worked for Elon across SpaceX and Tesla and elsewhere for a long time have been rewarded, both financially and in terms of their careers and what they've been able to accomplish." A well-defined culture filters for the right talent more effectively than any set of premium perks. The wrong employees will drift out of an organization of their own accord if the company clearly and consistently communicates its vision for the future and the nature of the road it intends to take. The ones who remain will be those eager to meet the challenges of that road, not despite but because of how steep it promises to be.

We met Dirk Robinson, engineering leader at Google and operating partner at Space Capital, in the previous chapter. Before Google, Robinson worked at Skybox Imaging on its revolutionary imaging satellite constellation.

"I joined Skybox Imaging when it was still in its early stage," Robinson told me. "That role gave me the opportunity to expand into space systems engineering, hardware design and manufacture, and large-scale computing." These would be valuable skills for any engineer, but learning how "to build and lead engineering teams and develop company culture," has proven more valuable to Robinson than any single technical skill he has developed.

Tech is always changing, but people work together—or fail to do so—in fundamentally similar ways. For a company to flourish in the Space Economy, getting the human aspects right is paramount. Unlike other areas of tech, the consequences of infighting and inefficiency go beyond website downtime or unhappy retail customers.

"Space is hard," Robinson told me. "There are a million things that can go wrong. The work spans a dozen engineering disciplines. The associated capital costs and lead times mean that failures are incredibly expensive." At Skybox, these difficulties were compounded by the realities facing any tech startup. "Tackling these challenges while also building a company on a shoestring budget added a whole additional layer of complexity."

What Robinson learned at Skybox wasn't simply how to drive everyone toward a particular milestone but how to create a system for a group of people to steadily achieve one milestone after another. "Seeing the 'first light' image from our first satellite gave me an incredible sense of accomplishment," he said, "but following that first launch with our second, launching our first constellation, and creating Skybox's operational mission systems revealed what I realized was an even bigger accomplishment: building an amazing team that could define and land ambitious goals."

Robinson's experience at Skybox prepared him well for his leadership role at Google: "A few engineering leaders and I set out to build a high-performing, inclusive engineering organization to launch and scale the Google Maps Platform," he told me. "We are a diverse engineering organization of highly talented engineering teams operating across multiple continents. Today, we provide mapping and imaging services to a billion users a month. As a team, we push each other to do great work while also looking out for one another. This culture of support played a crucial role in our ability to stay productive through the pandemic."

Muon Space continues to successfully attract top performers in a historically tight talent market. What's their trick to attracting the best and brightest?

"Partially luck," CEO Jonny Dyer told me, "but Muon's mission is extremely compelling to people. One of the strongest pulls is the desire to work on something impactful in the climate arena. It's such a big problem." Mission matters, but so does a shared appreciation for an intellectual challenge, something Dyer observed working at Skybox Imaging: "It's not about who's right and wrong. Everyone's in this to come up with the best solutions. That kind of culture builds on itself in a way that people can sense. It's energizing."

Seeing the culture grow organically at Skybox showed Dyer what was possible. "I've been striving to find ways to build those types of environments," Dyer said. "When hiring, our intention is to build a team of people we love to work with. When you get really smart people who are all in the mission together for the right reasons, it creates momentum. Smart, motivated people want to work with other smart, motivated people. This builds on itself in an exponential way."

"Even when people come in to interview," Dyer said, "they comment on this energy, the sense of shared mission, the shared belief in what we're doing." Creating an environment that is so palpably different is crucial to attracting the in-demand engineering, software, and science talent Muon and its competitors desperately need to reach their full potential.

As a leader in the Space Economy, you can't afford to direct all of your attention toward today's challenges. Things are moving too quickly. One of a CEO's most important roles is to articulate a vision for the future, and the future of the Space Economy is all too rapidly becoming its present.

***

The real action in the Space Economy today is almost entirely in the three tech stacks of the Satellite industry and what those stacks enable across the global economy. Launch itself represents only a small slice of the pie relative to these three stacks. Even as GPS, Geospatial Intelligence (GEOINT), and Satellite Communications (SatCom) soundly dominate the market, however, four Emerging Industries are gathering momentum in the distance. Today is not their day, but ignore them entirely only at your peril.

Likewise, there are larger threats and opportunities, from climate change to the militarization of space, worth the consideration of every professional in the Space Economy. In the next chapter, we will dispense with the hype and assemble a clear, fact-based, and reasonably balanced view of the future of the Space Economy. Where might it go from here?

CHAPTER 10

The Future of the Space Economy: What Happens When Orbit Is Cheap, Easy, and Safe?

Predictions are never perfect. That said, I'd like to use this last chapter to offer Space Capital's view of the road ahead. Nobody has a crystal ball. As thesis-driven investors, however, our most crucial function is the combining of expertise and imagination to identify likely outcomes. Whether or not your professional work or investments directly concern the Space Economy, it's a safe bet that we will all depend on space technologies in increasingly fundamental ways.

To be clear, nearly everything of consequence in today's Space Economy is happening in Satellites and Launch. Looking ahead, however, we can observe hints of four Emerging Industries, each offering varying degrees of long-term potential. For now, it isn't time to commit. Simply to pay attention. However, things may get interesting in one or more of these areas soon enough.

Before looking more closely at the four Emerging Industries as well as the threats posed—and potentially solved—by space tech, it's important to understand the linchpin of all next-generation efforts: Starship.

The Next (Really) Big Thing: Starship

Many venture-backed space companies of the last couple of years promised wonderful solutions—for a pre-Starship world. Despite the hype, many will be obsolete once the new SpaceX launch vehicle becomes operational. For years now, Space Capital has focused its attention only on companies that will leverage what Starship offers as opposed to those it will make redundant.

So, why is Starship such a game-changer?

For its first four decades, launch was constrained by cost (price per kilogram), upmass (payload mass carried to orbit), and payload volume (physical space available for a payload). These limiters kept orbit out of reach for all but major governments and defense contractors. Even those entities were enormously constrained in what they could send up.

Commercial viability improved when new, more powerful rockets like the Ariane 5 series emerged in the 1990s, enabling some of today's important legacy space companies. Then, SpaceX's Falcon 9, which entered commercial service in 2009 and pioneered reusability in 2015, brought the cost of orbit crashing down, ushering in a wave of innovation and freeing even tech start-ups from Earth's gravitational pull.

Falcon 9 also spurred competition. Other launch providers entered the marketplace, increasing supply and diversifying customer options. During this period, many pioneering companies began taking advantage of low-cost access to orbit by launching satellite constellations of unprecedented quantity and capability. This enabled the development of a new generation of capabilities across the three Satellite technology stacks: GPS, Geospatial Intelligence (GEOINT), and Satellite Communications (SatCom).

Phase 2 of the Space Economy will begin in earnest with the arrival of Starship, a revolutionary launch vehicle that promises to shake up all the givens of space—namely, that it's expensive, difficult, and dangerous to get there, that everything you launch must be purpose-built, engineered, and tested for years, and that every ounce matters.

If successful, Starship will be "the world's first fully reusable transportation system designed to carry both crew and cargo to Earth orbit, the Moon, Mars, and beyond."[1] With its stainless-steel construction, Starship will be affordable to build and affordable to launch. Affordable not on the scale of First World nation-states but of midsized corporations and even startups.

Starship is the tallest and most powerful launch vehicle ever built.[2] Launching from Starbase, SpaceX's launch site in Texas, Kennedy Space Center in Florida, or one of two planned offshore platforms,[3] the Super Heavy booster will bring a Starship spacecraft—carrying cargo, human crew, a Lunar lander, or a fuel tank—to low-Earth orbit (LEO). The second stage can then be refueled with liquid methane by orbiting tankers for trips to higher orbit or beyond. With Starship's mind-boggling capacity of one hundred tons, listing new applications that should be made possible by it dwarfs the imagination. Regardless of the mission, at its end Starship will land vertically, at which point both stages can be quickly prepared for another trip.

When you look at technological innovations that affect the global marketplace, only a handful in any generation cause paradigm-changing disruption—the cargo container reshaping world trade, for example, or the transistor unlocking Moore's Law and giving birth to the Information Age.

We believe Starship belongs in this Earth-shaking category. With new technology, it is always too easy to underestimate what lower cost and greater ease of use can enable.

While SpaceX's Falcon 9 opened up orbit to a broad swath of smaller customers, its cargo capacity—145 cubic meters—is a pittance compared to that of Starship. With the ability to carry one hundred tons that fit within 1,100 cubic meters for essentially the cost of fuel alone, Starship will completely change how we operate in space.

Consider the James Webb Space Telescope. Much of the cost and complexity involved with creating that amazing instrument came down to designing and building a mirror that could fold up for launch and then deploy once in orbit. With Starship, you could build and launch the same mirror with no folding required. The entire process would have been cheaper, faster, and easier—with superior results.

With Starship, you will no longer need to push the envelopes of performance, weight, or reliability to the limit without regard for cost. Once you can routinely launch large and heavy things into orbit and beyond, you no longer have to painstakingly carve away every superfluous ounce, design finicky origami structures of mind-bending complexity, or incorporate quadruple redundancy into every component. You can take risks and iterate. You can dispense with pristine clean-room conditions and build and assemble components in normal factories. After all, if one satellite in a constellation fails because of a speck of dust, it's only one of many. If you want, you can put your entire satellite manufacturing operation in orbit, too, keeping it fed with regular launches of raw materials. That way, you'll never run out of satellites.

Starship will transform our economy profoundly, but its potential goes beyond ferrying cargo to orbit and back like the Space Shuttle did. In Chapter 2, we saw how Polaris—the North Star—aided human navigation for thousands of years. It makes sense that the first set of planned crewed Starship missions are called Polaris. SpaceX even has a NASA contract to bring human crews to the Moon. Starship's landing craft could one day serve as our first permanent base on the Lunar surface. The vehicle may even bring the first human visitors to Mars.

Emerging Industries: An Overview

Nearly all equity investment into the Space Economy over the past decade has been made in Satellites and Launch. See Figure 10.1. However, a percentage point or so of $250 billion is still over $2 billion. Where has all that money gone? And how will the ongoing distribution of capital shift as Starship demolishes launch constraints and removes the barriers to entry and experimentation for new ideas?

We are beginning to see founders raise capital and build businesses focused on four Emerging Industries: Stations, Lunar, Logistics, and Industrials. Based on our data, $2.7 billion has been invested in these Emerging Industries over the past decade, with 41 percent of that invested in 2021 alone. Recently, this investment has been driven largely by venture capital firms, many of which are investing in the category for the first time. The majority of rounds are also seed and Series A, highlighting just how early we are in the development of these nascent areas of opportunity.

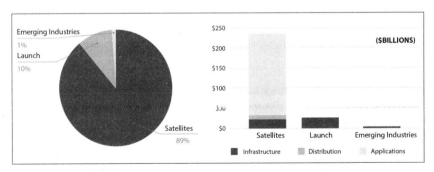

FIGURE 10.1 Cumulative Equity Investment in the Space Economy by Industry and Technology Layer 2013–2022

The geographic breakdown in Emerging Industries is also noteworthy. As in other market categories, the United States continues to account for the majority of investment, but Japan makes up a good third of the total. In fact, roughly half of all equity investment into Japanese space companies has been in the Emerging Industries, a clear indication of where Japanese founders are looking to make their impact in the Space Economy.

While overall venture momentum in the Space Economy keeps setting all-time records, plenty of that capital is still chasing solutions based on the decade-old Falcon 9 launch paradigm. With Starship expected to come online soon, we are entering a new phase. Investors—let alone entrepreneurs and career professionals—need to recognize that. Starship will fundamentally change the economics of space, further reducing cost-to-orbit, enabling Emerging Industries, and making existing infrastructure obsolete. As investors in this category, we're looking for founders building for this new reality.

Stations

Looking beyond the niche potential of short, suborbital flights for "space tourism," investors are expressing a growing interest in the possibility of permanent outposts in Earth's orbit.

The main problem with space stations is their expense. The International Space Station (ISS), for instance, cost an estimated $150 billion to build[4] and requires an annual $3 to $4 billion to maintain.[5] In fact, Guinness World Records calls the ISS the "most expensive man-made object."[6] Shaped by market forces, a private station might be more affordable, but could the effort of building one ever be worthwhile?

Hundreds of millions of dollars have been invested in the idea of commercial space habitats so far. Whether your plan is a private replacement for the ISS or a low-gravity amusement park, Starship will render these envisioned habitats obsolete before they reach orbit. If Marriott one day wants to box up a four-star hotel and send it to space aboard a launch vehicle, they'll have to assemble it in orbit. Instead, why not kit out the vessel's own interior with luxury accommodations on Earth and launch it already open for business? Marriott could even send its first round of guests aboard the vehicle and already checked into their rooms. Starship, in other words, can *be* the station.

Regardless of how stations end up being financed and built, or the commercial needs they will ultimately serve, there will be more activity in the decades to come involving not only creating stations but also providing them with supplies and other services.

Lunar

We use *Lunar* as a catchall term for commercial efforts both on and around the Moon: stations in Lunar orbit, landers, rovers, and bases on the surface. When a commercial Mars mission becomes a reality, it will begin as an expansion of this market.

Fifty years after Apollo 17 left the lunar surface, activity in this particular Emerging Industry is waxing once again. NASA's 2020 budget request prioritized Moon missions while emphasizing the role it sees private companies playing in achieving its objectives. Similar to the COTS program that gave rise to SpaceX, NASA's Commercial Lunar Payload Services (CLPS) contracts allow it to partner with commercial companies in its Lunar efforts. The Artemis program includes a precursor mission that will scout an ideal location for a Lunar base using Astrobotic robots followed by human lander missions using Starship to carry humans to the surface.

The private sector is a vital part of NASA's revamped Lunar focus. Though the Artemis program has encountered technical issues and delays, there is no question that NASA's emphasis on the Moon has spurred a boom in commercial Lunar activity and funding, much to the benefit of an array of ambitious startups—and to technological progress in general.

Given the low-gravity environment, the Moon may serve as a useful launch pad and refueling station for deep space missions. This will create a range of other opportunities for businesses and investors. NASA may become just one of many customers in a thriving marketplace as private companies provide spacecraft, vehicles, habitats, supporting systems, infrastructure, communications, and much else to a range of government and commercial Lunar operations.

Logistics

Logistics is the art of managing complexity. If there's one thing you can count on in the Space Economy, it's an abundance of complexity to manage. This Emerging Industry comprises three key functions: space traffic management, debris mitigation, and on-orbit servicing.

There is an ever-increasing need for better ways to avoid collisions and otherwise coordinate activity in orbit, whether above the Earth or around any other planetary body. Earth's orbit, of course, is already getting busy. In 2010, 74 satellites were launched into space. Ten years later, the Satellite Industry Association reported nearly 1,200—a 16-fold increase—and projected rapid growth from there.[7] As of this writing, there are well over 4,000 active satellites in orbit, with estimates of as many as 100,000 more in the decade to come.[8] Worse—from a debris perspective, anyway—active satellites represent only one percent of the overall mess up in LEO. Defunct satellites, discarded rocket stages, debris from collisions, remnants of weapon tests—it's getting dangerously crowded up there.

Our portfolio company LeoLabs has the best data on space traffic and debris. A spin-out of Stanford Research Institute, the company operates a network of ground-based radars that observe orbit for the purposes of both debris avoidance and space traffic control. Governments and private companies alike rely on this data for space domain awareness.

For debris removal, some start-ups have raised funding around complex and cost-prohibitive approaches to gathering up and disposing of defunct satellites and discarded rocket stages. Again, however, this is an area in which Starship changes the equation. Who needs a clever but complex approach to removing objects from orbit when Starship can do garbage pickup on its way back to the surface? After all, it will involve very little additional effort or marginal cost.

The final part of logistics is on-orbit servicing. The rapidly growing world of satellites above our heads will need plenty of repair work and refueling on an ongoing basis if we expect all these marvelous new services to remain steadily available. Maintenance is an inextricable part of healthy infrastructure no matter how much redundancy you have. Again, there is no predicting what on-orbit servicing will look like in a Starship-enabled future.

Industrials

Moving your factory into orbit provides unique advantages—high vacuum and low gravity, among others—to certain fabrication processes. Today, pharmaceutical companies are conducting research and development aboard the ISS, and ultra-high-quality fiber-optic cable is being manufactured there for specialized purposes. As launch costs drop, manufacturing other products in orbit, such as silicon chips, may make more commercial sense. There are other intriguing possibilities as well, such as 3D-printed human organs that, in the absence of gravity, wouldn't require scaffolding to hold their shape.

Combine all of this with the possibility of extracting resources from the Lunar surface or even passing asteroids and the possibilities multiply. If you're building a power plant or a communications tower for use on the Moon using raw materials that were mined in space, it makes little sense to bring everything down to Earth's surface for assembly before launching the finished piece into orbit. This is doubly true of massive structures that would be impractical to launch in Earth's gravity at all.

NASA considers "in-situ resource utilization" an essential component of future exploration efforts: "The farther humans go into deep space, the more important it will be to generate products with local materials."[9]

How would extraterrestrial mining work? In theory, mining the Moon should be relatively straightforward. Basalt, iron, quartz, and silicon—all present on the Lunar surface—could be extracted to construct permanent structures, among other uses.

The feat of landing a robot on an asteroid, using it to collect a small amount of material, and returning it to Earth has already been accomplished. The Japanese space agency, JAXA, completed two successful missions of this type: Hayabusa and Hayabusa2. In 2020, NASA also pulled it off, landing its OSIRIS-REx spacecraft on the asteroid Bennu, where it collected under a kilogram from the surface.

A single asteroid might contain an abundance of an element in short supply—or, at least, not within easy reach—on Earth. Many advanced electronics, including electric vehicles and other crucial green tech, are manufactured using increasingly rare elements. A mission to the right extraplanetary body might provide years' or even decades' worth of one of the metallic rare-Earth elements, like neodymium or terbium, used in some electric vehicle motors, helping us meet our ambitious green tech goals.

Much work remains to be done to make extraplanetary mining and manufacturing a practical reality. As key resources such as rare-Earth elements are exhausted on our surface, the economic viability of off-world mining will go up. Time will tell how quickly that point is reached.

Another long-term sector within Industrials is energy generation and storage. Space-based solar power has many advantages over ground-based panels like the ones you might have on your roof: no atmospheric absorption of light, no clouds, no night. Until now, the technology's potential has been limited by launch costs, but as those costs come down—and the demand for green energy goes up—the math looks better and better. Projects to develop space-based solar power are underway around the world.

Ensuring Peaceful Commerce and Cooperation in Space—and on the Surface

In 1959, the United Nations General Assembly established the Committee on the Peaceful Uses of Outer Space (COPUOS). COPUOS went on to create the 1967 Outer Space Treaty, an international agreement that has been signed by over 100 countries, including the United States, China, and Russia.

"The Outer Space Treaty of 1967 has allowed for the case of peaceful coexistence," Major General Michel Friedling, head of the French Joint Space Command, said at a recent international aerospace summit, "and bridges were made between East and West during these decades. But space is and will remain a key factor of economic strategy and military advantage for those who master space and those who know how to use space services. So, tensions on Earth will reflect in space."[10]

The 1967 treaty was written at a time when space posed very little practical value to nation-states. The first satellite, Sputnik 1, had only gone into orbit 10 years earlier. Times have changed. Just as technological developments during the Age of Sail, which extended from the sixteenth to the nineteenth centuries, transformed Earth's oceans into a global platform for both trade and conquest, the evolving Space Economy creates new threats even as it offers new opportunities. The ways that governments and private organizations cooperate to prevent conflict will have enormous long-term consequences for us all.

There is an urgent need for intelligent policies, laws, and treaties that reflect the reality of today's Space Economy. In no other way can we ensure the peaceful and profitable use of space and its resources by every country. Thankfully, there is no need to start from scratch. Society benefits from a large and robust body of international maritime law that enables global trade and bolsters world peace. While there are key domain differences, these generally accepted beliefs and precedents can help lawmakers and politicians frame a coherent, collective response to the unique needs of space. The right approach will ensure that companies and countries can operate harmoniously and profitably in Earth's orbit and beyond for the foreseeable future.

As previously stated, space is the invisible backbone of the global economy. Its importance to world trade is already foundational. Thus, it is in every nation's interest to work together to protect it.

The Future of "Star Wars"

In Chapter 3, I referred to two-time U.S. Secretary of Defense Donald Rumsfeld and his infamous "known unknowns." Verbal contortions aside, Rumsfeld shaped U.S. space policy in important ways over many decades. As Secretary of Defense under Gerald Ford, for example, Rumsfeld pushed for greater cooperation between NASA and the Department of Defense—both Skylab and the Shuttle program can be traced to this effort. Years later, before returning to the Secretary of Defense role under President George W. Bush, Rumsfeld chaired the Commission to Assess the Ballistic Missile Threat to the United States followed by the Commission to Assess United States National Security Space Management and Organization. The findings of these commissions have been enormously influential.

Before the commissions, President Bill Clinton had redirected America's antimissile research toward defenses against short-range missiles used on the battlefield. By that point, the once-omnipresent possibility of a long-range missile attack from the Soviet Union seemed like a distant memory. In 1993, as America celebrated the end of the Cold War, investing tens of billions of dollars in a ballistic missile defense system like Brilliant Pebbles, which involved placing thousands of heat-seeking missiles in orbit to strike down Russian ICBMs, struck lawmakers as a dangerous waste of resources.

At the end of that decade, however, long-range missiles still threatened the continental United States. China and Russia—already tilting in a troubling, new direction—could each land biological or nuclear payloads on American soil. Iran, North Korea, and even Iraq might be able to do so in a few years. Worse, the United States would have little warning before one of these missiles arrived. The commissions found that the U.S. intelligence community underestimated the odds of such an attack. If the United States didn't establish a ballistic missile shield of its own, whether that involved Strategic Defense Information Organization (SDIO)-style space lasers or some other technology, it faced the possibility of a "Space Pearl Harbor."[11]

Many experts downplayed these findings, but subsequent rocket demonstrations by North Korea and Iran caught the U.S. intelligence community by surprise, reinforcing the possibility that America was ignoring a genuine possibility. Though the United States still lacks a missile shield, Rumsfeld's efforts helped get the ball rolling for what eventually became the Space Force.

Time will tell how prescient any warnings about ballistic missile attacks on the United States were. The United States may one day restart some version of the "Star Wars" program envisioned by the Reagan Administration. But missile warfare itself represents only a small part of the larger story of how advances in space technology are changing the nature of combat.

The pivotal importance of satellites to national security is now all too obvious. In April 2021, U.S. Army General James H. Dickinson, head of the U.S. Space Command, told the Senate that space domain awareness was the command's number-one priority.[12]

That November, before Russia invaded Ukraine, it performed a successful antisatellite (ASAT) weapon demonstration, making clear that it possessed the ability to obliterate mission-critical GPS and Earth Observation (EO) satellites. As it turned out, LeoLabs provided accurate data on Russia's ASAT test several days before anyone else—including the U.S. government. Since LeoLabs is currently the only large-scale, commercial source of data and services for LEO, it represents a unique opportunity to augment and complement existing national defense space domain awareness assets.

Just as LeoLabs gives us an unparalleled understanding of the skies, Maxar, Planet Labs, and BlackSky offer essential EO data from above. Since the invasion of Ukraine began, these companies have created a foundation of truth for what is happening on the ground. Unexpectedly, the challenge for the intelligence community hasn't been in gathering enough EO data but in gleaning timely and actionable insights from the flood of information it receives from commercial satellite constellations. This is another problem several of our portfolio companies are working to solve.

Communications play a key role in any conflict. In a public-private partnership with the United States Agency for International Development (USAID), SpaceX has delivered thousands of Starlink terminals to Ukraine, ensuring that Ukrainians have a resilient communications pipeline.[13] Russia's preferred tactic of blocking messages in and out of a war zone has proved too difficult, allowing Ukraine to combat Russian propaganda and better fight the information war, even as its soldiers rely on Starlink internet to coordinate their operations.

An article in *Politico* described one Ukrainian soldier's experience using Starlink: "When planning a counterattack or artillery barrage, he dials up his superiors for last-minute orders via a rectangular white-and-gray Starlink satellite receiver concealed in a shallow pit in the garden of an abandoned cottage."[14] Starlink access isn't just about keeping military communication lines open, either. Thanks to SpaceX and the U.S. government, soldiers' friends and family can find out whether their loved ones are safe with Starlink even when the local cellphone network is down. As crucial as the billions of dollars of conventional military aid from the West have been—from rocket launchers to ammunition—the Starlink terminals serve as an essential "lifeline" for beleaguered Ukrainian forces.

Ensuring the Resilience of Space Infrastructure

Clearly, satellites will play a decisive role in all foreseeable conflicts. They are also enormously vulnerable to disruption. In April 2022, U.S. Vice President Kamala Harris announced the country's commitment against performing orbital ASAT tests.[15] An international coalition against the practice is currently forming. Though in all likelihood Russia would not choose to join such a coalition, the U.S. commitment alone still represents a major step forward. Not only are ASAT tests dangerously provocative, but they also create clouds of debris with the potential to damage space infrastructure and even endanger crews. The Russian ASAT test alone created over 1,500 trackable objects.

Theatrics aside, obliterating satellites wouldn't be necessary to disrupt an enemy's access to their data. For example, signals from every Global Navigation Satellite System (GNSS) are vulnerable to jamming. Considering how crucial satellite navigation technology has become to warfare, let alone our daily commutes, the need for a more diversified and resilient set of options for both military and civilian navigation has become obvious. GPS, meanwhile, is just one major problem area for commercial space companies to address in terms of national security. Threats are everywhere, which means addressable problems abound for innovative organizations.

"China is building military space capabilities rapidly, including sensing and communication systems, and numerous anti-satellite weapons," U.S. Space Command head General Dickinson told the Senate and House Armed Services Committees.[16] "All the while, China continues to maintain their public stance against the weaponization of space."

Satellites aren't the only infrastructure under threat. In response to Western sanctions, the Russian Space Agency chief at the time threatened to end 20 years of cooperation on the ISS. Without the Russian segment, he said, the ISS would lose its orbit and crash into the United States or Europe. (Thankfully, SpaceX indicated that its Dragon cargo spacecraft could prevent that.)

The traditional mindset of the military has evolved quite a bit since Donald Rumsfeld's day. The U.S. Space Force takes a broad view of providing space capabilities to American military forces at sea, air, and on the ground by relying on commercial capabilities that can be deployed more rapidly and cost-effectively than traditional systems. The Russia–Ukraine conflict is only accelerating innovation that was well underway. The strategic value and importance of the Space Economy will only continue to grow.

Adapting to a Changing Climate with Space Technology

Regardless of the degree to which you believe climate change is anthropogenic, there is no longer any doubt that the change itself is real. The important question facing governments, businesses, and the scientific community is: What can we do about it? More specifically, how will climate change progress, what are the main drivers of it, and which activities might slow or otherwise mitigate the effects of that change on our way of life?

Only space technology offers us the information we need to address these questions. This is why Lori Garver, whom we first met in Chapter 6, founded Earthrise, a philanthropic organization dedicated to using satellite data to support the fight against climate change.

"My thirty-five-year career in aerospace has never been about the rocket," Garver told me. "It's been about what space can offer us as a society. What space can do for humanity. One of the first benefits of going to space was the perspective that astronauts have always brought back to us: 'We live on a very fragile planet.' Now, because we've been able to reduce the costs—of getting to and from space, building satellites, modeling climate data, and storing massive amounts of data—we possess a far greater understanding of the Earth. I'm excited to understand more about what is happening to the planet and actually do something about that for future generations."

Temperature extremes, droughts, wildfires, and destructive weather events become more frequent and severe each year. These phenomena pose genuine threats. One study projects a loss of 18 percent of GDP to the world's economy by 2050 if no mitigating actions are taken.[17] Meanwhile, leading organizations are increasingly motivated by the environmental concerns of their stakeholders: customers, competitors, and shareholders. As a result of these strong incentives to better understand the climate risks associated with business assets, operations, and supply chains, large enterprises are setting ambitious goals.

Microsoft, for example, has committed to becoming carbon negative by 2030: "This means reducing our greenhouse gas (GHG) emissions by more than half, removing the rest, and then removing the equivalent of our historical emissions by 2050."[18] Meanwhile, 30 major asset managers, including Fidelity International and UBS Asset Management, announced in 2020 the goal of "achieving net zero carbon emissions across their investment portfolios by 2050."[19] Because these firms oversee

$9 trillion in assets in total, this decision promises an enormous impact over the coming decades.

Given the magnitude of the challenge, adapting to a changing climate is something we will have to work on collectively as a society: governments, businesses, and individuals. In this fight, the Space Economy has always played an outsized role. We wouldn't even know about climate change as a global trend if it weren't for satellite data. Moving forward, climate scientists agree that satellites are by far the best way we have to gather the information we need to guide policy. Over half the climate variables essential to our climate response can only be measured from space.[20]

Satellites have played a key role in our understanding of Earth's changing climate from the beginnings of the Space Race. In March 1958, the United States launched Vanguard 1, the first satellite to produce upper atmospheric density measurements. The Landsat satellite constellation that followed, beginning with the launch of Landsat 1 in 1972, provides the longest continuously acquired collection of space-based land remote-sensing data. More than half a century later, data from Landsat serves a range of applications in agriculture, forestry, mapping, geology, hydrology, coastal resources, and environmental monitoring.

Landsat and other, more recent efforts are just the beginning of what space can offer us in the fight against climate change. As the commoditization of launch services, satellite components, and cloud computing lower the barriers to entry for entrepreneurs, a wave of new companies is entering the arena. Some, like GHGSat, Muon Space, and MethaneSAT, mentioned earlier in the book, help organizations monitor and manage emissions. San Francisco's Pachama is building a forest carbon market using machine learning and satellite imagery to quantify carbon captured by forests. Regrow is helping farmers ensure a resilient food chain while minimizing water and fertilizer use. These are just a handful of the many promising directions being explored.

Today, a lack of independently verifiable direct measurement prevents climate markets from scaling. Meaningful measurements will create scalable markets. Data from thousands of new, ever-more-sophisticated EO satellites will pour into the cloud to be processed and interpreted by smarter and smarter AI to address the specific needs of industries ranging from agriculture to energy to transport to waste management. New applications will help businesses improve their operations and the financial sector price externalities like emissions and pollution.

All of this space activity raises another question: how much do rockets themselves pollute? In terms of emissions, launch contributes only a fraction of a percentage point of what the airline industry adds to the atmosphere. Meanwhile, rocket manufacturers are experimenting with more efficient engines, as well as cleaner energy sources like methane, where water would be the primary exhaust product. In reality, the greatest environmental impact of the Launch industry comes not from rocket exhaust but from the manufacturing and disposal of the rockets themselves. By introducing partial reusability with Falcon 9, SpaceX leaped forward on this front. The fully-reusable, methane-powered Starship promises even more progress in dramatically reducing the emissions involved in space travel.

We're just beginning to explore the Earth-saving potential of the Space Economy. With a growing satellite data infrastructure, entrepreneurs can focus on building specialized applications for tackling the many parts of this complex phenomenon without having to develop their own hardware. This is why equity financing for climate tech hit new highs in 2021. We expect that trend to continue.[21] In fact, we see a trillion-dollar investment opportunity in addressing climate change.

The market is still in an early stage, but the flywheel is starting to spin. A combination of government, commercial, and philanthropic initiatives promise to expand our understanding of Earth's systems and enable continual improvement in predicting future changes. The unifying goal of these programs is to identify a set of generally accepted scientific markers that can be independently validated to establish a transparent and accountable global climate market. The challenges created by climate change require a global perspective, and space technology will be a key building block of this new climate market.

Save the World—or Flee It?

The Space Economy evokes dystopian and utopian visions of the future. Many see space as our salvation, but few agree on how. Will we save our climate—and, by extension, ourselves—by spotting fugitive methane with EO satellites? Or is the long-term plan to escape a doomed planet by spreading across the solar system, as Elon Musk hopes to do? Luckily, we don't have to choose. We can pursue both options.

Climate change and war aren't the only threats we face. Remember the dinosaurs? As Musk is quick to point out, our options are to colonize other planets or keep all our eggs in one basket. From supervolcanoes to massive solar flares, there are a host of plausible Armageddon scenarios that are statistically unlikely in the near term yet practically inevitable over a long-enough time span.

It's easy to observe the protective quality of Earth's atmosphere. Just look at the difference between our surface and the crater-pocked face of the Moon. That said, asteroids large enough to penetrate our atmosphere and land with devastating effects are numerous in the Solar System. According to the *New York Times,* scientists estimate that there are 25,000 near-Earth asteroids large enough to pose a major threat. Sixty percent of these remain undetected. Since any of these rocks would hit Earth's surface with at least the force of "hundreds of millions of tons of TNT," new approaches to identifying incoming asteroids will be instrumental in what NASA calls "planetary defense."

To address this threat, Dr. Ed Lu, physicist, former NASA astronaut, and co-founder and vice president of Strategic Projects at LeoLabs, helped found B612 Foundation, a non-profit using data analysis to spot large, Earth-bound asteroids with enough years of advance warning to potentially deflect them. Originally, B612 had planned to finance and build its own space telescope. When that proved financially difficult, the organization pivoted to an algorithmic approach that would have been unthinkable two decades ago. Recently, B612 announced that it has discovered more than a hundred new asteroids using computational analysis of preexisting images in the archives of the National Optical-Infrared Astronomy Research Laboratory.[22]

Using algorithms to locate asteroids by analyzing existing telescope images is exactly the kind of thing made possible by freeing vast amounts of data from central archives and making them more available for civilian and academic use. Dr. Lu and B612 were aided in their efforts not only by the image data but also by access to the computational power required to crunch all that data, in this case contributed to the cause by Google. Since the new asteroids were discovered by analyzing only a small slice of the available image data, B612 estimates that tens of thousands can still be found without capturing a single additional image. None of these rocks may be headed toward Earth, but if a single one is, we will be grateful for the advance warning.

What will we do with a warning if we get one? To test one approach to planetary defense, NASA conducted the Double Asteroid Redirection Test, "the first-ever space mission to demonstrate asteroid deflection by kinetic impactor."[23] On September 26, 2022, the DART spacecraft, launched by a SpaceX Falcon 9 in November 2021, successfully struck a distant asteroid—one with no chance of striking our planet—with colossal force. As it happened, DART shifted the asteroid's orbit three times as much as scientists had hoped.

"If an Earth-threatening asteroid was discovered and we could see it far enough away, this technique could be used to deflect it," NASA Administrator Bill Nelson told the *New York Times*.[24]

Finally, is the vision of a permanent human presence on the Moon or even Mars feasible? It's not just possible but, judging by progress on key efforts across the Space Economy, likely. As a species, we will soon embark on a journey to the Moon and beyond, scattering ourselves so widely that no calamity could ever threaten all of us at once. In the meantime, there are exciting and lucrative opportunities right now for entrepreneurs, investors, and aspiring professionals to improve life on this planet—and secure our survival as a species.

Conclusion

In 2012, I decided to start a firm focused on investing in the Space Economy. SpaceX launched to the ISS for the first time that year, not long after launching its first customer successfully. The timing of Space Capital seemed obvious to me, if not to my friends and family.

After laying the groundwork, Space Capital launched its first fund in 2015. In 2017, after years of collecting information on start-up and investment trends in the Space Economy, we began publishing our insights in our *Space Investment Quarterly*. When we first shared our views on the Space Economy publicly, it was still a relatively unknown phenomenon, even in the business world. The reception to our output was immediate: people were interested in hearing more.

In addition to our quarterly reports, we have published several thesis papers: "The GPS Playbook," "The GEOINT Playbook," "The SatCom Playbook," "The Great Climate Opportunity," and others. Although this all involves much work, we're eager to do it and grateful for the receptive audience. It's been clear from the beginning of our information-sharing efforts just how effective a fact-based, carefully vetted perspective can be at clearing away misconceptions, hype, and flat-out misinformation. Sunlight is the best disinfectant.

My goal in writing this book has been to take the work we've been doing with our research publications, as well as our other efforts at public education, to the next level, bringing all our best thinking about the Space Economy and its potential together in one place.

Ultimately, I hope this book has convinced you of the once-in-a-generation importance of this extraordinary phenomenon while dispelling the harmful myths that crop up incessantly around it. It's the nature of any hot new market to attract irrational enthusiasts, skeptics, and snake-oil sellers. If I've struck a reasonable, evidence-based middle ground that holds up to the scrutiny of industry veterans and other genuine experts, it was only through the help of my fine colleagues and this book's many contributors.

Is there money to be made in the Space Economy? Absolutely. SpaceX, Skybox, and others have already created meaningful ROI for founders, employees, and investors, and we're still in the early innings. If we weren't firmly convinced of the potential of the Space Economy and the infinite array of groundbreaking, world-changing products, services, and other opportunities already spinning out from it, we would never have come together to create Space Capital. Whether you're an investor, an entrepreneur, or an aspiring professional, you owe it to yourself to participate in this growth.

That said, I'm most interested in convincing you of the potential impact that you can make by planting your stake here. It's still early days, but not so early that the possibilities are in any way limited. The category is growing exponentially, which means that opportunities abound. Investors have put $260 billion into 1,700 space companies over the last 10 years as ambitious founders seek product-market fit across the six Space Economy industries and the three technology layers of Infrastructure, Distribution, and Applications. As of this writing, aspiring professionals can choose from among 30,000 jobs across 700 companies on our Space Talent job board alone, with roles ranging from engineering to marketing to IT to design.

Beyond all this, the Space Economy offers every human being the all-too-rare opportunity to have an outsized positive effect on our world. What would you do if someone sent you back to 1995 with everything you know—good and bad—about what the World Wide Web would eventually become? How would you use your intelligence, talent, experience, and expertise to help guide that rising phenomenon in a better direction?

"Give me a lever long enough and a fulcrum to place it," Archimedes said, "and I will move the earth." It is my belief that the Space Economy is such a fulcrum, a place from which anyone can achieve extraordinary things for all of humanity. What you do with this opportunity is up to you, but consider this book a clarion call to seize it.

Notes

Epigraph

1. "Christa McAuliffe and Barbara Morgan: The First Spaceflight Participants Discuss Teaching and the Program," *NASA Lyndon B. Johnson Space Center Space News Roundup* 24, no. 22 (December 6, 1985), p. 3.

Introduction

1. Michael Sheetz, "An Investor's Guide to Space, Wall Street's Next Trillion-Dollar Industry," *CNBC* (blog), November 9, 2019, https://www.cnbc.com/2019/11/09/how-to-invest-in-space-companies-complete-guide-to-rockets-satellites-and-more.html.
2. Mary Meehan, "Trends For 2022: Change the Way You Look at Change," *Forbes* (blog), December 21, 2021, https://www.forbes.com/sites/marymeehan/2021/12/21/trends-for-2022-change-the-way-you-look-at-change/.
3. Rupert Neate, "SpaceX Could Make Elon Musk World's First Trillionaire, Says Morgan Stanley," *The Guardian*, October 20, 2021, sec. Technology, https://www.theguardian.com/technology/2021/oct/20/spacex-could-make-elon-musk-world-first-trillionaire-says-morgan-stanley.
4. Josh Friedman, "Entrepreneur Tries His Midas Touch in Space," *Los Angeles Times,* April 22, 2003, https://www.latimes.com/archives/la-xpm-2003-apr-22-fi-spacex22-story.html.
5. Rebecca Boyle, "The New Race to the Moon," *Scientific American* 37, no. 2 (August 2022): 72–77; updated as "A New Private Moon Race Kicks Off Soon," https://www.scientificamerican.com/article/a-new-private-moon-race-kicks-off-soon/.
6. Chad Anderson, "Rethinking Public–Private Space Travel," *Space Policy* 29, no. 4 (November 1, 2013): 266–271, https://doi.org/10.1016/j.spacepol.2013.08.002.

7. Stephen Clark, "World's Rockets on Pace for Record Year of Launch Activity," *Spaceflight Now* (blog), July 6, 2022, https://spaceflightnow.com/2022/07/06/worlds-rockets-on-pace-for-record-year-of-launch-activity/.

Chapter 1: Space Is the Next Big Thing: To See the Future of Your Job, Your Investments, and the Economy, Look Up

1. "Economic Benefits of the Global Positioning System (GPS)" (RTI International, June 2019).
2. "First Comes an Electric Car. Next, a Trip to Mars," *Wall Street Journal*, June 2, 2013, sec. Special, https://online.wsj.com/article/SB10001424127887323728204578515743066949964.html.
3. *60 Minutes,* "2012: SpaceX: Elon Musk's Race to Space," 60 Minutes Rewind, 2018, https://www.youtube.com/watch?v=23GzpbNUyI4.
4. Nadia Drake, "Russia Just Blew Up a Satellite—Here's Why That Spells Trouble for Spaceflight," *National Geographic* (blog), November 16, 2021, https://www.nationalgeographic.com/science/article/russia-just-blew-up-a-satellite-heres-why-that-spells-trouble-for-spaceflight.
5. Roger D. Launius, "First Moon Landing Was Nearly a US–Soviet Mission," *Nature* 571, no. 7764 (July 2019): 167–168, https://doi.org/10.1038/d41586-019-02088-4.
6. "NASA Commercial Crew Program: Significant Work Remains to Begin Operational Missions to the Space Station" (United States Government Accountability Office, January 2020).
7. Larry Press, "Update on China SatNet's GuoWang Broadband Constellation—Can They Do It?," *CircleID* (blog), February 3, 2022, https://circleid.com/posts/20220203-update-on-china-satnets-guowang-broadband-constellation-can-they-do-it.
8. "FAQ," Equatorial Launch Australia (ELA), accessed June 28, 2022, https://ela.space/faq/.

Chapter 2: Mapping the Space Economy: Understanding the Ecosystem and Its Key Players

1. Kathryn Schulz, "When Shipping Containers Sink in the Drink," *The New Yorker,* May 30, 2022, https://www.newyorker.com/magazine/2022/06/06/when-shipping-containers-sink-in-the-drink.
2. Fortune Business Insights, "Geospatial Analytics Market Size, Growth | Global Report [2028]," 2021, https://www.fortunebusinessinsights.com/geospatial-analytics-market-102219.
3. DigitalGlobe Case Study, 2016, https://aws.amazon.com/solutions/case-studies/digitalglobe/.
4. Arthur C. Clarke, "V2 for Ionosphere Research?," *Wireless World*, February 1945.

Chapter 3: Chief Orbital Officer: Profiles in Space Economy Entrepreneurship

1. Wendy Whitman Cobb, "How SpaceX Lowered Costs and Reduced Barriers to Space," *The Conversation* (blog), March 1, 2019, http://theconversation.com/how-spacex-lowered-costs-and-reduced-barriers-to-space-112586.
2. "Full profile: Dr Anastasia Volkova CEO and Co-founder, Regrow," Australian Government Department of Industry, Science and Resources (Department of Industry, Science and Resources, October 5, 2021), https://www.industry.gov.au/australian-space-discovery-centre/people-in-the-space-sector/full-profile-dr-anastasia-volkova-ceo-and-co-founder-regrow.

Chapter 4: No Overhead: How and Why to Start a Business in the Space Economy

1. Renée A. Mauborgne and W. Chan Kim, *Blue Ocean Strategy: How to Create Uncontested Market Space and Make the Competition Irrelevant* (Harvard Business Review Press, 2014).
2. David Brandt-Erichsen, "SpaceX Comments on Successful SpaceX Launch," *National Space Society* (blog), May 22, 2012, https://space .nss.org/spacex-comments-on-successful-spacex-launch/.

Chapter 5: Charting a Trajectory: Co-founders, Customers, and Capital

1. Peter F. Drucker, *Management: Tasks, Responsibilities, Practices,* Kindle edition (HarperCollins, 2009).

Chapter 8: Navigating Space Careers: Seizing the Opportunity of a Lifetime

1. "Meet Patti Grace Smith," Patti Grace Smith Fellowship, accessed October 5, 2022, https://www.pgsfellowship.org/meet-patti.
2. Nancy Kathryn Walecki, "A Course for the Commercial Space Age," *Harvard Magazine*, March 15, 2022, https://www.harvardmagazine. com/2022/03/hbs-commercial-space-age-course.

Chapter 10: The Future of the Space Economy: What Happens When Orbit Is Cheap, Easy, and Safe?

1. SpaceX, "Polaris Program," Polaris Program, accessed September 9, 2022, https://polarisprogram.com/.
2. Jonathan Amos, "Biggest Ever Rocket Is Assembled Briefly in Texas," BBC News, August 6, 2021, sec. Science & Environment, https://www.bbc.com/news/science-environment-58120874.
3. Chris Bergin, "Frosty Texas Vehicles and Groundwork in Florida Ahead of Starship Evolution," *NASASpaceFlight.Com* (blog), March 6, 2022, https://www.nasaspaceflight.com/2022/03/texas-florida-starship-evolution/.
4. Claude Lafleur, "Costs of US Piloted Programs," *The Space Review* (blog), March 8, 2010, https://www.thespacereview.com/article/1579/1.
5. Office of Inspector General, "NASA's Management and Utilization of the International Space Station," NASA (July 30, 2018).
6. Guinness World Records, "Most Expensive Man-Made Object," Guinness World Records, accessed September 19, 2022, https://www.guinnessworldrecords.com/world-records/most-expensive-man-made-object.
7. Rachel Jewett, "SIA Report Highlights Record-Breaking Number of Satellites Launched in 2020," *Via Satellite* (blog), July 12, 2021, https://www.satellitetoday.com/business/2021/07/12/sia-report-highlights-record-breaking-number-of-satellites-launched-in-2020/.
8. Nathaniel Scharping, "The Future of Satellites Lies in the Constellations," Astronomy.com (blog), June 30, 2021, https://astronomy.com/news/2021/06/the-future-of-satellites-lies-in-giant-constellations.

9. NASA, "In-Situ Resource Utilization," April 6, 2020, http://www
.nasa.gov/isru.

10. Sarwat Nasir, "UAE Chosen to Chair UN's Committee on Peaceful Uses of Outer Space," *The National,* June 1, 2022, sec. UAE, https://www.thenationalnews.com/uae/2022/06/01/uae-chosen-to-chair-uns-commitee-on-peaceful-uses-of-outer-space/.

11. John A. Tirpak, "The Space Commission Reports," *Air & Space Forces Magazine*, March 1, 2001, https://www.airandspaceforces.com/article/0301space/.

12. U.S. Space Command Public Affairs Office, "USSPACECOM Commander Discusses Space Domain Awareness, Operating Environment of Space at Senate Hearing," U.S. Space Command, April 21, 2021, https://www.spacecom.mil/Newsroom/News/Article-Display/Article/2580511/usspacecom-commander-discusses-space-domain-awareness-operating-environment-of/.

13. Cristiano Lima, "Analysis | U.S. Quietly Paying Millions to Send Starlink Terminals to Ukraine, Contrary to SpaceX Claims," *Washington Post,* April 8, 2022, https://www.washingtonpost.com/politics/2022/04/08/us-quietly-paying-millions-send-starlink-terminals-ukraine-contrary-spacexs-claims/.

14. Christopher Miller, Mark Scott, and Bryan Bender, "UkraineX: How Elon Musk's Space Satellites Changed the War on the Ground," *Politico,* June 8, 2022, https://www.politico.eu/article/elon-musk-ukraine-starlink/.

15. Bruce McClintock, "U.S. Decision on ASAT Testing a Positive Step Towards Space Sustainability," *The RAND Blog* (blog), April 21, 2022, https://www.rand.org/blog/2022/04/united-states-decision-on-asat-testing-a-positive-step.html.

16. U.S. Space Command Public Affairs Office, "USSPACECOM Commander Discusses Space Domain Awareness, Operating Environment of Space at Senate Hearing," *U.S. Space Command,* April 21, 2021, https://www.spacecom.mil/Newsroom/News/Article-Display/Article/2580511/usspacecom-commander-discusses-space-domain-awareness-operating-environment-of/.

17. Swiss Re Group, "World Economy Set to Lose up to 18% GDP from Climate Change If No Action Taken, Reveals Swiss Re Institute's Stress-Test Analysis," Swiss Re Group, April 22, 2021, https://www.swissre.com/media/press-release/nr-20210422-economics-of-climate-change-risks.html.

18. Microsoft, "Microsoft Carbon Dioxide Removal Program," Microsoft Sustainability, accessed September 19, 2022, https://www.microsoft.com/en-us/corporate-responsibility/sustainability/carbon-removal-program.

19. Attracta Mooney, "Fund Managers with \$9tn in Assets Set Net Zero Goal," *Financial Times*, December 11, 2020, https://www.ft.com/content/d77d5ecb-4439-4f6b-b509-fffa42c194db.

20. World Economic Forum Global Future Council on Space Technologies, "Six Ways Space Technologies Benefit Life on Earth," September 2020.

21. Silicon Valley Bank, "The Future of Climate Tech 2022," 2022.

22. Kenneth Chang, "Killer Asteroids Are Hiding in Plain Sight. A New Tool Helps Spot Them," *New York Times*, May 31, 2022, sec. Science, https://www.nytimes.com/2022/05/31/science/asteroids-algorithm-planetary-defense.html.

23. NASA, "DART Mission Overview," DART, accessed September 19, 2022, https://dart.jhuapl.edu/Mission/index.php.

24. Sarah Scoles, "NASA Spacecraft Accomplishes Mission and Smashes Asteroid Into New Orbit," *New York Times*, October 11, 2022, sec. Science, https://www.nytimes.com/2022/10/11/science/nasa-dart-asteroid-spacecraft.html.

About the Author

Described by *TechCrunch* as "among the best-positioned people on either the investment or the operator side to weigh in on the current and future state of the space startup industry," Chad Anderson is the founder and managing partner of Space Capital, where he has been pioneering investment in the Space Economy for over a decade.

Regularly featured in the media as an expert, Anderson has appeared in outlets including CNBC, Bloomberg, CNN, the *Wall Street Journal*, the *New York Times*, and the *Financial Times*. In addition to his work at Space Capital, Anderson serves on boards including that of the Satellite Applications Catapult, which supports the United Kingdom's national strategy to grow its space sector.

Anderson has served as director of the board of the Explorers Club, a nonprofit that promotes the scientific exploration of land, sea, air, and space. He was also a member of the User Advisory Committee for the International Space Station U.S. National Laboratory.

Before founding Space Capital, Anderson led a successful career at JPMorgan Chase, where he managed a $50-billion real estate portfolio through the Great Recession. He has an MBA with a focus on entrepreneurship and innovation from the University of Oxford.

Anderson lives in New York City with his wife, Radhika. An avid explorer in his free time, Anderson was among the first people to swim the circumference of the island of Islay, Scotland. Stopping at each of the island's operating distilleries and filling a 30-gallon oak cask with whisky from each, he bottled and sold the resulting blend to benefit the Royal National Lifeboat Institution. Anderson also mapped the ancient mezcal trail in Oaxaca, Mexico, transporting a 50-gallon oak barrel of actively fermenting agave pulp across the state and, in the process, creating the world's most unique mezcal.

Index

experiences, 157–158
guide, 165
process, 172–176
Regrow, 39–40, 78
EO data, combination, 70
examination, 69–72
impact, sustainability, 88
investor question, 104–105
sensor fusion, power
(demonstration), 72
software, usage, 71
Regulators, engagement
(importance), 131–132
Relationships, importance, 162–163
Remote sensing data, applications
integration, 60
Remote work, problems, 169–170
Rendered.ai, 37, 81, 132, 150
founding, 82
Repeater stations, usage, 41
Retention
employees (retention), culture
(importance), 177–180
guide, 165
Reusable first-stage rockets, usage, 51
Ring security system, reliance, 43
Robinson, Dirk, 155–158, 162, 178
Rocket Development Corporation
(RDC) (Universal Space Lines
subsidiary), 120
Rocket Lab, 12, 20
product teams, leadership, 93
ships, creation, 26
Rockets, pollution capability
(question), 199
Rohrschneider, Reuben (Dyer
connection), 97
Rothenberg, Joe, 118, 159
Roulette, Joey, 136
Rumsfeld, Donald, 75–76, 192–193, 196
Runway
pivoting, 105
securing, 103

S

Safire Partners, 157, 173
Satellite-based sensors, Muon Space
development, 62
Satellite Communications (SatCom), 10,
22f, 40–44

advantages, 21
antenna deal, 81
applications, 44
distribution, 42–44
infrastructure, 42
smart buoys, potential, 79
use cases, growth, 139–140
Satellites
constellations, determination, 58
data, access, 62
detail, providing, 67
health, reporting, 59
image patterns, algorithms (usage), 79
imagery, usage, 71
Industry matrix, incumbents/
upstarts, 80
innovation, 27–38
objective data, Arbol reliance, 67
technology stacks, 12
usage/ranking, 22f
weather data, incorporation, 39
Schingler, Robbie, 51–53, 65, 75,
94–95, 154
talent, attraction (difficulty),
165–166
venture capital, usage, 103
Schmitt, Jack, 16
Schulz, Kathryn, 26
SeeMe (LEO satellite constellation), 152
Selective availability, 29
Sensor data, Muon data platform, 63
Sensor fusion
economic potential, 78
power, Regrow demonstration, 72
Series C growth capital, raising, 11
SES (Luxembourg), competition, 42
Sheetz, Michael, 136
Signal, noise (distinguishing), 1
Single-stage-to-orbit, reusable launch
vehicle (SSTO RLV), McDonnell
Douglas development, 116–117
Skills
demands, higher education lag,
148–149
importance, 156–157
Skybox Imaging, 34–35, 155, 158
Google, relationship, 34
lessons, 178–179
operational mission systems,
creation, 179